What Matters Now

WHAT MATTERS NOW

ROY JENKINS

COLLINS/FONTANA
1972

First published 1972

© Roy Jenkins

Printed in Great Britain by
Love & Malcomson Limited
Redhill, Surrey

Contents

Author's Note

The main part of this book is based on a series of speeches which I delivered to Labour Party and Trade Union audiences between March and September 1972. I have made only a few alterations, mostly to cut out references strictly for the occasion, or to bring a figure up to date.

In preparing them I have been greatly helped by a number of people, most of all by Mrs. Judith Marquand. Her contribution has been invaluable. Mr. Matthew Oakeshott and Mr. Nicholas Bosanquet have also been of special assistance. In addition, a number of my colleagues in the House of Commons have been very generous with their time and advice, as have several outside experts, who have been consulted on particular points. The responsibility throughout, both for facts and views, is of course exclusively my own.

R.H.J.
September 1972

The Call to Idealism

More than two years have passed since the last election. They have been bad years for the nation. The Conservatives have impoverished the public services, widened the gulf between rich and poor and helped to create a meaner, more selfish and more dangerously tense society. Every Labour platform in the country has reverberated with denunciations of Conservative policies and Conservative outlook. But although it is necessary and right that we should expose the limitations of the present Government, that is only the beginning of our duty as a movement of conscience and reform.

When the next election comes, we shall not be judged by the vehemence of our perorations, still less by the dexterity with which we follow the transient twists and turns of public opinion. We shall be judged by the quality of the programme we put before our fellow citizens, and by the consistency and courage with which we advocate it. If we are to carry more conviction with the electorate than we carried in 1970—if, above all, we are to sustain a more effective assault on poverty and injustice than we launched between 1964 and 1970—we must use our period in opposition to hammer out a coherent and credible strategy of social progress, capable of winning support, not only from our own ranks, but from a majority of the society around us. To be worth pursuing, such a strategy must be based on the ideals for which this movement has stood since its foundation. To carry conviction, it must be rooted unmistakably in the realities of Britain in the 1970s.

What are these realities? They are a mixture of the good and the bad. This is still one of the more civilized and agreeable countries in the world in which to live. We are materially far better off than most of the world. No-one can come back from the crushing poverty and misery of Bengal, as I did in early 1972, and exaggerate our problems. Yet it is precisely because we have been lucky both in our history and in our current framework of opportunity that it is so inexcusable that we allow the persistence in Britain of hopelessness and deprivation. Just because it could be avoided, the poverty of the old, the widows, the deserted, the low paid, the large families of this country are a greater reproach to Mr Heath, or indeed to myself, who was a Minister in a recent Government, than are the hundreds of thousands who live and die upon the pavements of Calcutta to Mrs Gandhi. Here people rarely die on pavements. But there are many whose hope dies, and dies understandably but unnecessarily, within their own homes.

I take an example from a constituency case. A woman asked me to go and see her in her council flat, as she was unwell and did not want to go out. In fact she was not too unwell to go out, but probably thought that her circumstances would make a greater impact on me if I saw them on the spot, rather than have them explained at my advice bureau. She was right. She was a deserted wife, aged about fifty. Her husband left her in 1966 and paid her a rather erratic £5 a week. She had one son who had recently married and left home. She had encouraged him to do so, in the hope that it would help his marriage to go better than her own. But it left her on the edge of destitution and permanent bitterness. He could not spare a penny for her as he was fully committed with establishing his own new home. He had taken his own bedroom furniture with him. She could not afford to replace it, nor that of the rest of the flat, which was depressingly dilapidated. Her total income was her maintenance payment plus £8.42 which she earned from a catering job in another part of Birmingham. But her tax deduction was £2.20 and her fares £1 a week. Her net income from her job was therefore £5.22. Was it worth working, particularly as it made worse her chronic bronchitis? But on the other hand not working and just sitting 'watching your walls' made worse her equally chronic depression. Certainly there was no point in hoping for a small rise. She had just had one—of 55p per week. It had gone straight off her rent rebate. I could find no useful advice to give her, Her problems were of course partly personal, but greatly exacerbated by a relentless penury. *She was caught in a real poverty trap.* What meaning for her had slogans like 'standing on your own feet' or 'improving yourself by your own efforts'?

That case is far from unique. Every Member of Parliament, every local councillor, every social worker has to deal with many similar cases—cases where an individual or group of individuals has been trapped by a vicious circle of misfortune and deprivation, where it has become impossible for the victim to break out of the trap unaided, where the appropriate social agencies have been unable to provide the aid, and where in consequence, he or she has become surrounded by a miasma of hopelessness.

The vicious circle does not operate only at the level of the individual. It also operates—equally harshly and equally unjustly—at the level of the localities in which we live. Lancashire children, for example, need schooling as much as children in other parts of the country. Lancashire parents are as willing to make sacrifices; Lancashire councillors are as eager to provide the services. Yet in 1970-71, Lancashire spent £4½ m. less on education than was needed to provide the expenditure per child equivalent to the average for the country. Each Lancashire child was nearly 10% less well-provided for than in the country as a whole. In the case of the child welfare services, the gap between what Lancashire spent per head and what the rest of the country spent was wider still. The reason is not just that Lancashire needs or wants less education or poorer child welfare services than the rest of the country needs or wants. The reason is that the product of a p rate per head in Lancashire is only about two-thirds of the average product in the country as a whole—and that Government grants are insufficient to close the gap. Children in Lancashire have a smaller chance of developing their talents, a smaller chance of acquiring higher education, and a smaller chance of equipping themselves with the skills that are increasingly necessary in the modern world than children in London and the South-East—not because they are less talented or less deserving, but because they have the misfortune to live in a poorer locality. Here, too, the weak get weaker while the strong gain strength.

These examples are not isolated or untypical. In spite of half a century of effort, our society—and still more our world—is still disfigured by gross unfairness which, without constant correction, feeds strongly upon itself. In April 1971, weekly earnings for men in full-time work averaged £32.30. Women in full-time work earned an average of only £17.80—not much more than half the figures for men. More than a hundred thousand men—and about two million women—earned less than £15 a week. In April 1970 nearly half the workforce in the West Midlands earned more than £30 a week: in East Anglia the figure was little more than a quarter. Inequalities of wealth are still more glaring.

These inequalities of income and wealth are reflected in, and still further buttressed by, a host of local and regional inequalities. In London, Camden, which includes some very prosperous residential areas, spends £190 a year per head of its population on publicly provided local services; but Wandsworth spends only £75 a year. In Wales, the urban district of Glyncorrwg, at the head of an old coal valley, can afford only £50 per head per year. But the rural district of Magor and St. Mellons, on the suburban fringes of Newport and Cardiff, spends £318 per head per year. Wisbech in agricultural Cambridgeshire spends less than £41. But Northwich in the residential part of Cheshire spends £153. Regional statistics tell the same story. Unemployment in Scotland is three times as high as in London and the South East. In Wales, more than half the children leaving school enter unskilled occupations. In the South East the proportion is less than a third.

Far too often, inequality is cumulative. The higher your income, the more likely it is that you possess inherited wealth —and that you, in your turn, will leave wealth to your heirs. The lower your earnings, the greater is your need for community services. But the more likely it is that you live in a poor locality which cannot afford to provide such services except on a niggardly basis.

This is even more obviously true of the world beyond our shores. Two-thirds of the world's population lives in countries which in 1967 had a national product per head of less than a third that of the United Kingdom. Some of the poorest countries, like India, had a national income per head of only about £30 a year. And their rate of improvement is less than that of the rich countries. The gap grows wider, not narrower. Some deny concern for far away countries of which we know little. When I wrote about Bangladesh several correspondents wrote and asked me why I worried about other people's problems rather than concentrating on our own. Most of them were pretty poor themselves. Their attitude was understandable. Yet I think it was wrong, even for their own immediate interests. Concern is invisible and so is selfishness. A society which says 'to hell with famine and disease in Bangladesh, it's all their own fault, isn't it' is extremely unlikely to balance this with compassion and justice for its own pensioners and its own low-paid. Superficially there may seem to be a contradiction between help for those in need abroad and help for those in need at home. It is not a real contradiction. Those who want help must not seek to deny it to others. It is the same current of opinion which will endeavour to help those in need both at home and abroad. And it is the same contrary current which will seek to ignore those all over the world who cannot stand on their own feet.

Most of the injustices we suffer from here at home have been exacerbated—sometimes openly, and sometimes covertly—by the present Government. As time goes on we can expect further steps along this road. Although few Conservatives still advocate inequality as a positive idea, the philosophy they espouse leads almost inevitably in that direction. At the heart of modern Conservatism lies a belief in the individual solution of economic problems. The individual is paramount. The fact that individuals live in society is largely forgotten or ignored. Freedom of economic choice is sacrosanct. In a complex, and highly interdependent society, policies based on such beliefs are almost bound to benefit the strong at the expense of the weak.

Individual freedom of choice if meaningful is highly desirable. I believe that one of the main tasks of the democratic left is to widen the area of human choice, and I shall always be grateful for the opportunities I had as Home Secretary to work towards that goal. Ironically many Conservative MPs who so strongly proclaim the virtues of individual freedom in the economic field, where it can do great harm to others, have bitterly resisted the growth of greater legal tolerance in the field of personal conduct, where individual behaviour rarely interferes with the rights of others. Many of them instinctively regard a young man with long hair as a greater enemy of society than a factory owner who pollutes a river.

But freedom of economic behaviour needs to be handled with far more care. If it is given primacy over all other values, and pursued without reference to social realities, the results are likely to be disastrous. For in a society like ours—subject to rapid and disorienting change, and characterized by harsh disparities of social power—millions of individuals cannot enjoy freedom of choice in any meaningful sense without constant and unremitting effort on the part of the community at large. Two hundred years ago, the pioneers of *laissez-faire* economics postulated a society composed of separate individuals, each pursuing his own individual well-being to the exclusion of all else, and each capable of making the choices that confronted him in a light of a rational calculation of advantage and disadvantage. In the real world such a society is simply inconceivable. Large numbers of our fellow citizens lack the knowledge to calculate the advantages and disadvantages of the choices they have to make. Many more lack the power to make the right choice at the right time.

To tell my deserted constituent in Birmingham—or, for that matter, an unemployed shipyard worker on the Tyne, or a coloured child in a dilapidated classroom in South London, or a low-paid worker in a Glasgow slum—that they have the freedom to choose a way of life for themselves, is, in a very real sense, to add insult to injury. It is an insult because it is untrue and everyone knows it is untrue. It is an injury because it fortifies complacency and diverts attention from the needs we ought to meet. The right to choose is meaningless without the power to choose; and in a society as riven by unfairness as ours still is, any approach to fairness, any approach to a real ability to choose, requires constant intervention by the state. In the real world, communal action is not the enemy of individual freedom, but its guarantor; the pursuit of individual economic freedom to the exclusion of all else may increase freedom for a few, but only by restricting the real freedom of the many.

The social forces that bolster inequality are immensely powerful—and immensely persistent. Left to themselves they would produce a society so intolerable as to be self-destructive within a decade. The pattern in which wage incomes before taxation are distributed has remained unchanged since 1886, the first year for which the Department of Employment has adequate records—in spite of trade unionism, in spite of universal education, in spite of two world wars and in spite of unprecedented technological change. In the 1950s, many of us thought the inequalities would diminish as society became more prosperous. It is now clear that this view was at best over-simplified, and at worst just wrong. Indeed, there is some reason to believe that the social and technical changes which accompany and make possible a faster rate of economic growth may even intensify inequality, unless strong countervailing measures are introduced.

The number of people living below National Assistance scales increased threefold between 1953 and 1960: as society as a whole grew richer, and the minimum standard which society considered to be adequate was raised a growing minority fell below that standard. In the United States, too, the incomes of some of the poorest groups—notably of farm families and of families headed by a woman or an older person—have fallen further behind the average. Families in these categories constitute only a quarter of the families in the population, but they include 60% of the poor families. Even in Sweden, the richest country in Europe, where the Social Democrats have been in power for a generation, a Royal Commission recently reported that inequality has not been significantly reduced and that a whole host of new measures would be needed to reduce it.

Yet this is not as surprising as it might appear at first sight. Society is not, and never has been, simply a collection of individuals. Individuals belong to groups; and strong groups load the dice in favour of their members. Big firms take over their competitors; a child born into a rich family automatically starts life with an advantage; strong unions force up the price of their members' labour. In the same way the weak have the dice loaded against them. As a result, the minority of those with very high incomes at one end of the scale, and the larger minority of those with very low incomes at the other end, are more numerous and further apart than they would be if rewards were determined solely by a combination of effort, enterprise and talent. The non-governmental institutions of our society as opposed to the state itself, mostly increase rather than diminish the natural inequality of reward. In addition, the market mechanism strengthens rich regions at the expense of poor regions, successful firms at the expense of small men, the well-organized at the expense of the badly organized.

But the persistence of injustice is not an excuse for complacency or a reason for despair. It is a challenge to be overcome. In a world in which the traditional bonds of habit, status and deference are rapidly dissolving, flagrant disparities of income, wealth and power are likely to pose an increasingly ominous threat to social peace. A hundred, even sixty years ago, 'the rich man in his castle, the poor man at his gate' both saw their respective positions in the social hierarchy as part of an immutable order, which only the impious or foolish would seek to change. A social order based on deference is no longer possible, and to radicals as well as socialists this must be a matter for rejoicing. But unless the old deferential order is to be replaced only by an accelerating social chaos, in which each group fights with increasing intransigence to defend its own, and in which the strong at all levels trample with increasing impunity upon the weak, we must strike a new and acceptable balance between economic reward and social merit.

If there are exceptional strains in society at the present time it is largely because there has been no significant change in this direction for a considerable time past. During the war and the years immediately following there was a very significant change. It was done under the shadow of a considerable austerity, which persisted, for most of the Attlee Government, and from which there was bound to be some reaction. Even so, when the reaction had taken place and when the second Churchill Government had been in power for two or three years there was still a rough approach to a balance between the social system then accepted and the distribution of rewards. It was no longer the old social system of pre-1939, still less of pre-1914 days. It was not based on an absolute distinction between the rights and expectations of the rich and those of the mass of the population. Even so there was in the mid-'fifties a considerable persistence of modified deference. It was still a world in which it was thought perfectly natural to create new hereditary titles, in which education was wholly dominated by the values and the supremacy of the traditional establishments, in which the young of different classes looked and dressed more like their parents than like each other.

Over the past decade and a half there has been a great further social change. The world of deference has only a few traces left. But there has been no corresponding shift during this period in the pattern of rewards. The poor are still poor. Property speculators—and some others—are as relatively rich as were those who used to have an accepted position at the top of the old social structure. The result, quite inevitably, is increasing social strain. It is as though we were still trying to run our air traffic control system on the flight patterns of 1956. That would be certain to produce an increasing number of very disagreeable incidents. The same danger now exists for our whole social system. We must correct it, not by allowing those with strong arms, at whatever level they operate, to have their way, but by creating a new and fairer balance which can freely be accepted and warmly defended by men of responsibility and goodwill throughout the community.

That is the only kind of order which will give us a new stability. It is the only kind of order which deserves to last. It can be built only on compassion and fair dealing. Gross and stubborn inequality is incompatible with it, and we cannot hope to bring it into being until we launch a major attack on the unjustified disparities that still divide us from each other. Some levelling down will be required, but levelling up is far more important. *The next Labour Government can be content with nothing less than the elimination of poverty as a social problem.* It is a formidable but not an insurmountable objective.

In the later essays I attempt a more detailed examination of the methods and the measures necessary to achieve this— measures to deal with unfairness between individuals, with unfairness between the localities in which we live, with unfairness between the regions, with unfairness between organized groups of employers and workers, and with unfairness between the nations. We can, however, learn something from the last Government. I reject the more extreme criticisms of its social policy. It did a good deal of which we can be proud. It made society more tolerant, more civilized, more compassionate. It narrowed slightly one of the worst poverty gaps, that between large families and the rest. It improved many vital community services. It made an important social advance with redundancy payments and earnings related unemployment benefits. And it always had to operate under the shadow of persistent inherited balance of payments weakness, which was cured only by an enormous switch of resources in 1968 and 1969. Yet the plain fact is, and I take my full share of responsibility for this, that not enough was done to change society and achieve our traditional objectives.

The main reason was lack of adequate, sustained economic growth. Only one year out of the six—1968—saw a satisfactory performance in this respect. Next time we must be resolved to do better. Apart from anything else the central need to return to full employment will dictate either this or a major revamping of patterns of work. And I believe that, freed of the daunting balance of payments deficit which we took on in 1964 and never got rid of until very near the end, it is strongly likely that we shall. Yet when we contemplate the failure in the growth field of successive British Governments—Tory, Labour, Tory—it is too easy a way out to say that we look to economic growth to solve all the difficult problems, helping those most in need and everything else. What is undoubtedly true is that with sustained growth we can level up both more rapidly and more acceptably than without it. But I am not prepared to let everything depend on growth. I want a strategy to deal with poverty if our hopes are fulfilled and the economy bounds along. But I want an alternative, fall back, inevitably less satisfactory but still effective strategy to deal with poverty if our hopes are again disappointed and growth is less than we would wish. This is not defeatism. It is making sure that those whose need is greatest are not merely the residual beneficiaries.

This involves facing up to some awkward facts. Ninety years ago, the pioneers of Fabian Socialism used to offer public lectures on the theme: 'Why are the many poor?' Today the many are not poor. The many, while far from rich, have an approach to comfort and some free spending money. The poor are a minority, but a very sizeable minority. And the hard fact is that, if the social forces that sustain injustice are to be offset, then the comfortable majority will have to make their contribution. It is an illusion to imagine that the gap between rich and poor and the rest of us can be closed solely at the expense of the very rich. The rich can and should make a disproportionate contribution, but it would be intellectually dishonest, and in the long run politically disastrous, to pretend that increased taxes on the rich can solve the problem altogether. Two years ago—all figures of this sort tend to be a little out of date—if the state had taken all incomes of more than £5,000 a year, the additional revenue at the Chancellor's disposal would have amounted to only about 1% of Inland Revenue receipts. If growth is rapid the problem is much eased. It is only a moderation of the general rate of advance which would be called for. But the possibility cannot be ignored that even if we escape the past errors of economic management we may still run up against real ecological dangers which will make growth not the ally but the enemy of civilization. And a country as wealthy as Britain ought to be able to remove the abuses of remaining poverty within approximately its present resources.

The Labour Movement was created to fight against a wealthy minority on behalf of a poor majority. Now it has a more complex and demanding task. It has to enlist the majority in a struggle on behalf of a poor minority, who on grounds of age or health or family circumstances or disgracefully low pay are unable to help themselves. It can only be done if it is shown that the problem of injustice cannot be dealt with piece-meal. No-one has a right to expect a fair deal for himself unless he is prepared to work for others too. To arouse a movement of opinion, which by blending good sense and social conscience will enable us to escape from the narrow and self-defeating sectionalism of which we have recently seen too much, requires not just a series of separate policies but the search for a coordinated strategy which will raise political sights, tap the latent idealism of the British people, and go to the heart of the problem of the free acceptance of a fair society.

The people of this country are rightly disillusioned with an incompetent Conservative Government, which is now at once nervous and complacent. But I do not believe that they will turn enthusiastically to us instead if we have no positive alternative to offer. On the contrary, I believe that unless we can demonstrate that we, at least, do not see politics as a mere game of 'ins' and 'outs', an arcane affair of House of Commons tricks and manoeuvres, public disillusionment with the present Government will spill over into a more general disillusionment with the parliamentary system itself. Cynicism about politics and politicians is already widespread. It is the deadliest single enemy of any party which wishes to change society through the ballot box.

But if our attack on injustice is to be effective it is not enough to devise an appropriate strategy. That is only the first step. It is also necessary to develop a relationship of trust and understanding with the electorate. For our strategy will succeed only if the majority supports it not merely on election day, but through the disappointments and vicissitudes which are bound to follow. We have to persuade men and women who are themselves reasonably well off that they have a duty to forgo some of the advantages they would otherwise enjoy for the sake of others who are much poorer than they are. We have to persuade motor car workers in my constituency that they have an obligation to low-paid workers in the public sector. We have to persuade the British people as a whole that they have an obligation to Africans and Asians whom they have never seen. It is a formidable task. We cannot hope to carry it out if we base our appeal on immediate material self-interest. Necessarily some of the measures we propose will run counter to the immediate interest of the majority. Nor can we trust to class loyalties of the traditional kind : the gulf between majority and minority now cuts across class lines. Our only hope is to appeal to the latent idealism of all men and women of goodwill—irrespective of their income brackets, irrespective of their class origins, irrespective in many cases of their past political affiliations.

The challenge of injustice, though centuries old in substance, has now taken on a new and more subtle form. To meet that new challenge we need a new kind of politics. Three centuries ago, the poet Andrew Marvell wrote of Cromwell

> . . . Casting the Kingdoms old
> Into another mould.

That is our task too. We have to break the mould of custom, selfishness and apathy which condemns so many of our fellow countrymen to avoidable indignity and deprivation. In place of the politics of envy, we must put the politics of compassion; in place of the politics of cupidity, the politics of injustice; in place of the politics of opportunism, the politics of principle. Only so can we hope to succeed. Only so will success be worth having.

The Needs of the Regions

On 10 January 1972, at Workington in the Cumberland coalfield, 1,945 people were out of work. The percentage of unemployment in Workington in January was 7.0—almost two-thirds as much again as the national average of 4.3%. Ten years ago, in January 1962, unemployment in Workington was almost 2½ times the national average. And 45 years ago, in January 1927—the first month for which detailed local figures are available—unemployment in Workington stood at 24.7% —twice the national average of 12% of the insured population.

I give these figures extending back over nearly half a century in order to illustrate from one town the stubborn persistence of regional inequality. Such inequality has many dimensions. Not only has unemployment in the Northern region as a whole remained at more than 1½ times the average percentage for Great Britain throughout the last decade, but average incomes per person and per household are about 10% below the national average. In 1969, 60% of the households in the United Kingdom owned a refrigerator, but only 48% in the Northern region. 51% of the households in the United Kingdom owned a car; in the Northern region the figure was 43%. In Great Britain as a whole, the average number of days of sickness per man at work was 15½; in the Northern region, it was 25½. In England, the average number of patients per dentist is 4,000; in the Northern region, one dentist serves on average 6,400 people.

Yet the Northern region is by no means the worst off. Unemployment is higher in Scotland and in Northern Ireland; incomes are lower in these regions—and also in Wales and in Yorkshire and Humberside—than they are in the North. In Wales, more than half the school leavers enter occupations with no further training. In the United Kingdom as a whole the proportion is only one-third. In Northern Ireland, less than 12% of 17-year-olds are still at school. In the North-West and in East Anglia, the figure is 14%, while in the United Kingdom as a whole it is more than 17%. In the South-East it is 20%. In the Northern region, and also in Yorkshire and Humberside and in the North-West, 15% of the homes are below the minimum acceptable standards. In the South-East only 6% of homes have been declared statutorily unfit.

These inequalities are not due to God-given differences in climate or natural resources. They are the result of human action—and even more of human inaction. Most of the poorest regions of today were the richest regions of yesterday or of the day before yesterday. In the early nineteenth century, industrial Lancashire was the wonder of the world; in the latter part of that century, when the navies of the world were fuelled with steam coal, the South Wales coalfield looked like an El Dorado to poverty-stricken workers across the Bristol Channel. My own grandfather was drawn from Somerset to the mines of Monmouthshire in the 1870s, and my father followed him into the pits, until, two years after I was born, he became a miners' agent and later a miners' MP.

These and similar regions declined later because coal, textiles and shipbuilding, on which their prosperity had been based, ceased to hold their own in world markets—and because Governments blinkered by the dogmas of *laissez-faire* economics failed to appreciate that they could not diversify into new and more competitive industries without help from the State. Private enterprise lacked the resources to renew the capital stock of the older industrial areas; even more disastrously, it lacked the initiative to adjust the pattern of their economic activities to the changing pattern of demand. The new industries, like automobiles and light engineering, that sprang up between the wars were located, not in old industrial areas like Durham, or South Wales or Lancashire, but in the Midlands and the South-East; unemployed miners who found jobs in these new industries had to leave their homes to do so. A vicious circle thus set in. Jobs were scarcer than elsewhere, and wages lower; the young and vigorous often drifted away in search of work; standards of health and housing—of communally provided-services and privately-provided amenities—declined in comparison with the country as a whole; the areas concerned became even less attractive to private enterprise than they had been before.

It is an old story now. But it has continuing lessons. For it has unmistakably emerged since the middle fifties that the forces which make rich regions richer and poor regions poorer—the forces which turned Jarrow and the Rhondda Valley into industrial deserts—are still in operation today. It is clear that in the absence of countervailing action by the State, growth becomes concentrated in a limited number of centres. The most successful firms—the firms which increase their shares of the market and their profits by responding successfully to changes in consumer demand—tend to locate themselves initially in the more prosperous regions, which because they are more prosperous provide bigger markets. Once established, such firms have a competitive advantage over firms starting later in less prosperous regions. Their greater cash-flow leads further and more quickly towards self-finance for their capital requirements. They can afford to invest more; and they can install more modern equipment. This enables them to increase their productivity. Greater productivity gives them a still greater advantage over firms elsewhere.

Meanwhile, capital flows out of the poor regions to the more prosperous ones. Private investors can earn a better return by investing in a successful firm in a prosperous region than by investing in a small and struggling firm nearer home. Many of the more prosperous elderly move out of the regions where they used to work to spend their pensions in resort towns. The flow of people of working age also runs away from the depressed areas. The unemployed leave their homes to find work elsewhere. Ambitious and able young people do the same; 43% of university graduates are employed in London and the South-East, although only 34% of the total labour force is there employed. Yet managers and workers whose actions help to make rich regions richer and poor regions poorer cannot be blamed, as individuals, for doing so. If workers cannot find work at home, they can hardly be blamed for finding work in a more prosperous region. An individual firm—whose management is responsible ultimately to private shareholders—cannot be expected to act singlehandedly in the common interest of the nation. Individual firms, like individual workers, are the agents of economic forces they cannot individually control. If their actions harm the common good, it is not they who should be blamed but the Government which has failed to channel economic forces into a healthier direction.

It is against this background that the present Government's new regional policies must be judged. The March 1972 measures demonstrated a remarkable conversion in this sphere. The decision to re-introduce the Labour Government's investment grants, so arbitrarily wound up only a year and a half ago; the more muted tone of the announcement that the regional employment premium (REP) would be phased out in place of the previous commitment to an abrupt cessation in 1974; the changes in the machinery of government—all these are welcome. Yet the new measures are much less radical than they may appear at first sight. The new Industrial Development Executive consists of part of the present Department of Trade and Industry, together with a division for small firms arising out of the recommendations of the Bolton Report. The intention to recruit some new staff from industry and the City is certainly not very novel. The Government has stolen some of our old clothes and has put them on with a mixture of brazenness and reluctance; it has made no new clothes of its own. Its retreat from the dogmas of 1970 and 1971 has been forced upon it by its own economic failures and the consequent fear of electoral retribution; it is the result of no genuine intellectual or philosophical conversion. The dogmas of *laissez-faire* have gone. The self-confidence of Mr Heath and Mr John Davies in the days when they intrepidly hunted the lame ducks of Britain has gone. In its place is a vacuum.

The ineffective turn-abouts of the present Government offer us an easy target. Let us by all means hit it. But that does not solve the problem. The Labour Government's regional policies, operated in very difficult circumstances, at least prevented regional inequalities from becoming more acute. It is no accident that unemployment in Workington was even higher in comparison to the national average in 1962 than in 1972. Under the Labour Government, the unemployment percentage in every planning region except East Anglia and the North moved closer to the national average. The same is true of average weekly earnings. The fact remains that the weapons we used between 1964 and 1970 did not and probably could not do the whole job. Industrial Development Certificates and Office Development Permits control development in the prosperous regions; they do not, in themselves, create new jobs elsewhere. When the economy is booming, they function well. At other times their effectiveness is reduced. Office Development Permits will have an increasingly important part to play as white-collar jobs in the service sector become steadily more numerous. But they are negative instruments, not positive ones.

Equally, the regional employment premium is likely to be decisively vindicated when the full studies of its effects become available. It has advantages which investment grants do not possess. It is not merely a stimulus to expansion or modernization, desirable though those are. It also helps to maintain existing employment by discouraging firms from moving away or closing down. In addition, of course, its relative advantage is much greater to labour intensive than to capital intensive industry. And in the areas of high unemployment, by definition, it is labour which is the factor of production in abundant supply. I do not want to keep capital intensive industry out of development areas. Any industry is welcome, and there is of course always some employment factor involved. Furthermore, a healthy and successful industrial area needs to contain some plants with vast advanced equipment and few men as well as labour absorbing assembly units. But it would certainly be perverse, where unemployment is the essential problem, to concentrate incentives upon machines rather than men.

A sustained regional employment subsidy, whether in the form of REP or of the reduced employers' national insurance contribution used in the South of Italy, will be a continuing need for a long time to come. In my view it should now be broadened, so as to include not merely manufacturing but the service industries as well. The tilt to these forms of employment is a strong continuing development in Britain as in all advanced countries. In the past ten years the numbers employed in manufacturing industry have increased by only 59,000 or less than 1%. In the same period the number employed in the three white-collar sectors of Insurance, Banking and Finance; Professional and Scientific Services; and Public Administration have risen by nearly 1,500,000 or almost 40%. The regions will never catch up unless they have a substantial share of this white-collar and service sector growth. It may indeed be the case that even such a traditionally prosperous area as the West Midlands may be at the beginning of transition to depression precisely because it is over-dependent upon manufacturing. Manufacturing as a whole, without an adequate service interlacing, may now be as unsatisfactory a foundation for prosperity as were the old basic industries fifty years ago. Yet in the poorer regions that interlacing is still weak. Over two-fifths of the office floor space in England and Wales is in Greater London.

A broader and continuing REP of this sort would enable the

regions to gain the sort of benefit which devaluation brings to an economy which has grown sluggish and laggardly. Its competitiveness is increased, its activity is quickened. But changes in currency parity are clearly quite impracticable within this country. They would produce hopeless confusion and disarray. A fully valued £ in London, a 90p one in Leeds and an 80p one in Newcastle is hardly an attractive prospect. Indeed it may well be the case that, as the world grows smaller, parity changes will become undesirable over wider areas It therefore becomes increasingly necessary to get the benefits for the weaker regions of the effects of internal devaluation by a more practical method.

It is also for the poorer regions a fairer method. Devaluation is always a cost in terms of resources. It is a stimulus but also a penalty. It means you get less, in terms of other currencies, for goods you sell, and pay more, in terms of your own, for those you buy. You escape from a strait-jacket but at the cost of paying a ransom to the rest of the world. If our only concern were with employment in the development areas this might not matter. But our concern is also with income distribution, with the fact that average purchasing power, unemployment apart, is less, significantly less, in the Northern Region, in Scotland, in Wales, than in London or the South-East or the Midlands. Greater competitiveness bought at the price of an income penalty would therefore help one part of the problem at the expense of the other. But REP, widened and perhaps varied, avoids this penalty. It is paid for by the country as a whole, and not merely by the poorer regions. It could be a practical, equally effective and much fairer substitute for regional devaluation.

So far I have been discussing measures which encourage the private sector to expand in the regions. These are important, but the evidence is that they are unlikely in themselves to do more than ameliorate the deep-seated and unacceptable disease of regional inequality. To secure the full balance of prosperity which has eluded us at least since the collapse of the post-

1918 boom signalled a longer-term decline of the old basic industries, requires more direct Government intervention. By this I do not mean that I want everything to be done from Whitehall. Even within the poorer regions a policy of indiscriminate, blanket growth is neither practicable nor desirable. It will be necessary to make decisions, often difficult ones, as to which local areas should be given priority for development. I would like these decisions, so far as possible, taken in the regions themselves. The people on the spot may often know better, and should in any event be able to decide, within the resources available from outside, exactly where it is best to go for resurgence or new development.

But the need for greater public activity as a whole is now clear. Government, acting through the public sector, can adopt a broader perspective than that of any board of directors nominally responsible to its shareholders. It can view an investment in a much longer time scale. It can estimate the benefit of an industrial development to the community as a whole, in terms of new jobs and better use of social capital. It can assess the profitability of any single project in the context of other linked developments. Often the scale of development required to provide the base for a new industrial complex is too great for any individual firm to take the risk. Perhaps most important of all, the Government alone can estimate the costs of inaction as well as of action. The problem of the regions will not be cured without more direct Government involvement and a greater use of public interprise.

Fifteen years ago, when national full employment seemed secure and regional inequalities could plausibly be regarded as a hang-over from the past rather than as a continuing problem for the future, it was widely thought that future extensions of public ownership would have more to do with equality than with economic control. Keynesian techniques, it was believed, could maintain full employment; and indicative planning could ensure balanced growth. Public ownership would no doubt be used from time to time, as one instrument among many; but its role in future would be much less central than it had been between 1945 and 1950 or than the pioneers of the Labour Movement had imagined. Time has again moved on, new problems have arisen and old ones have reasserted themselves. It is now clear that techniques for managing the whole economy cannot solve detailed problems—even when the problem is that of a whole region rather than a single firm. General demand management must be supplemented by more rigorous policies of direct intervention than those which we used between 1964 and 1970. We relied principally on a mixture of bribery and cajolery—on lavish grants supplemented by some Government pressure on the more public spirited or politically exposed businesses. These weapons were far better than no weapons at all and their results should not be underestimated, but they have not nearly solved all the problems which we face in this field of regional policy.

For too long the question of public ownership in Britain has been dominated by dogma from both sides. The performance of our nationalized industries, especially in terms of productivity, has been outstandingly good by comparison with our other industries, and also good by comparison with the corresponding industries in other countries. Between 1958 and 1968, output per man in manufacturing rose in this country by 3.7% each year on average. In no nationalized industry except buses was the rise less than 4%—a rate exceeded in the private sector only by the isolated cases of chemicals, textiles, bricks and cement. The average for the public enterprise sector was 5.3%. Nor is this to be explained away by a disproportionately favourable allocation of new capital to the public sector. After making allowance for this factor, productivity in electricity, coal, gas, the railways, BEA and BOAC, all rose by as much or more than the average for the manufacturing sector. Our coal industry is as efficient as that of any East or West European country except perhaps for Germany; in railways, efficiency is only clearly behind Holland, with Germany as a marginal case; in airlines it is slightly less than that in Germany, Holland and Italy, but above France, Belgium, Scandinavia and Switzerland. Unlike our manufacturing productivity, with a growth rate which puts us lowest of all European countries and almost at the bottom of the league table, the growth of productivity in all our nationalized industries ranks well in international comparisons.

Because our nationalized industries have been managing their affairs rather well over the last ten or fifteen years, they have built up a pool of able managers. In view of this record, it is both foolish and discreditable that the present Government should seek to hive off parts of the nationalized industries and return them to the private sector. We should move firmly in the other direction. We should seek to hive on parts of the private sector to the nationalized sector, and encourage the nationalized sector to diversify wherever it sees a good opportunity.

But the fact, both here and abroad, all indicate that the remorseless pressures of a highly industrialized economy lead towards the need for greater public ownership. It was the complexities and cost of the RB 211 engine that forced this Government to nationalize Rolls Royce. It would be highly irresponsible for the Government, now that it has invested the taxpayers' money at high risk in rescuing Rolls Royce, to carry out its doctrinaire promise of selling the company back to private ownership as soon as its economic prospects are fair enough to make investors believe that they could achieve a satisfactory return on their investment. It is manifestly equitable as the Labour Party said over 10 years ago in "Signposts for the Sixties", that 'Where national assistance is required by manufacturing industry, it should be made conditional on public participation in the enterprise'.

The myth that only private ownership has the managerial ability, entrepreneurial flair and marketing skills to run modern industry dies hard in Britain. Yet, experience abroad in the highly competitive motor car industry certainly does not bear this out. Renault, wholly Government owned, competes

only too effectively with our own cars, even in this country.
And the French Government has been able through a national
policy of industrial location to build a major new plant to
boost local employment in Normandy. Alfa Romeo with new
plants opening in Southern Italy, is wholly owned by the
Italian National State Holding Company, IRI. Volkswagen
was Government owned throughout its formative years of
mounting success. Its change to a private company has co-
incided as it happens with the onset of a period of relative
decline.

In Holland, Dutch State Mines, a limited company wholly
owned by Government, has established, in partnership with
DAF, the Born car works at Limburg. where coalmines have
been closing since 1965. The Born works alone employ 6,000
people in a district where mine closures made 8,000 workers
redundant. Dutch State Mines has entered into partnership
with other firms in Limburg; it has also been expanding its
own chemical interests in the area and now employs more
workers in chemicals than in mining. In addition, it has provided finance to private firms which needed risk-bearing capital in order to undertake projects in Limburg. Indeed it pursues
a wide-ranging policy of diversification, and of partnership
with and participation in private sector projects, to minimize
the hardships arising from a programme which will close down
the last Limburg coalmines in 1975.

Italy has extensive experience with State Holding Companies. IRI (Industrial Reconstruction Institute) is the older; it
was founded to prevent certain important banks from ruin in
the inter-war financial crisis; their portfolios provided the basis
from which, with Government financial support, it has gradually reached the position where it controls firms in banking,
mining, ship-building, merchant shipping, chemicals, telephone
services, airlines, radio and television services, civil engineering, and the manufacture of motor vehicles, industrial equipment, and many other products. ENI (Ente Nazionale Idro-
carburi) was founded in 1953 to 'manage and carry out initia-

B

tives of national interest in the fields of hydrocarbons and natural gases'. It produces and distributes oil and natural gas, and transports, refines and markets petroleum products. In addition, it has now diversified into nuclear energy, textiles and engineering. All in all, IRI and ENI control some 370 companies, from Motta and Alemagna in food processing, to oil refineries and steel mills. Moreover, since 1968 the Italian Government has decreed that all new projects undertaken by the State Holding Companies should be in the Italian Development Area, the South. 60% of gross investment undertaken by the Holding Companies has to be located there.

By any objective standard, British investment has remained obstinately sluggish over at least two decades. In any international league table, the proportion of the British national product spent on investment occupies much the same lowly position as the British rate of growth. Even with the strong regional policies which prevailed between 1964 and 1970, this small quantity of investment was not channelled sufficiently to the regions to produce acceptable reductions in regional unemployment. Despite the IDC policy, industrial floor space increased faster than the national average in the South-East and the two Midland regions from 1964-7. Britain needs an investment stimulus, and especially a stimulus in the regions, that a major State Holding Company is ideally fitted to provide. Such a company would be a flexible vehicle for direct Government involvement to help achieve the broad-based mix of activities which is essential if the regions are to receive their fair share of national prosperity. The Holding Company could be supported by a Regional Development Bank equipped with substantial initial resources, which would make loans on specially advantageous terms. It would deploy its funds flexibly over the development areas to help a host of the smaller scale manufacturing and service industries such as tourism which are managed by private enterprise.

It is not sufficient for the regions simply to receive new satellite factories from the Midlands or the South-East. Such satellites are often the first to suffer in a recession. Nor can we rely on revamping older industries—shipbuilding, mining and textiles. We must turn our attention to new potentialities —the oilfields around our coast for example, or the effects for our ports and their hinterlands that the changing patterns of trade associated with entry into the Common Market may bring. Government has already taken an active part in locating aluminium smelting, power and petro-chemical plants in the regions, but these are all capital intensive industries which employ relatively few people. The manufacturing industries which have a high proportion of labour in relation to their output include the whole wide range of the engineering and motor vehicle industries, together with hosiery and other clothing, pottery and glass, furniture, pharmaceuticals, and one or two others. It is in such industries that direct government involvement could be decisive in bringing new vitality to the regions.

It was worth examining the Italian experience with State Holding Companies, not because the situation is directly comparable, but for what it can show us about the practice of active state intervention in a mixed economy. For if a State Holding Company is to be effective, it has to represent a broad spectrum of industry. Only in this way can it afford to adopt an unusually long time scale for some of its projects, or to take risks too large for most ordinary companies to contemplate. Subject only to special subsidies where the State Holding Company is asked to undertake a clearly unprofitable venture for social reasons, it should be expected to operate like any commercial undertaking and to earn profits. Its diversity would enable it to spread its risks.

The State Holding Company would have to grow steadily from the base provided by existing public holdings in private industry. Its scarcest resource is likely to be the supply of experienced yet adventurous management. It is this which is likely to set a limit to its rate of growth. But there is already a solid base; we own 49% of BP, now the largest and among the most profitable of British companies. We own 100% of

Rolls Royce; we have a stake in International Computers Ltd. and in a number of other companies. These, supplemented by a limited amount of selective nationalization, should provide a good base from which to diversify into the labour-using industries which the regions require. To embark on its extensive programme of acquisition and diversification, the State Holding Company would require finance. This should come partly from its own profits, partly from Government grants, and partly from the capital market.

Since the fulfilment of the 1945 Government's programme of basic nationalization, I have always believed that public ownership should be judged more by the results it will produce than by abstractions and preconceived views. I have not been convinced that it contains the key to the elimination of injustice between individuals. I think we need other weapons for that. Nor do I think it necessarily solves the problem of injustice between different groups of workers. The hard struggles which have had recently to be fought for tolerable wages in the public sector—not least in the mining industry—is evidence of that. But I am increasingly convinced that injustice between the regions cannot be dealt with except by a significant expansion of the public sector. And I am equally convinced that our society will be permanently blemished so long as there are sharp divisions in employment levels, in income levels, in standards of living, in opportunity for professional advancement without deserting areas of origin, between different parts of the country. This will be a divisive force, regionally and nationally, within the United Kingdom. If the South is allowed to suck away a disproportionate share of our country's prosperity there can be no real national cohesion. It will not even be good for the South itself. It will there lead to increasing congestion, even strangulation of the arteries of tolerable living, to mounting destruction of the amenities of life, which in the last resort are the central concern of our programmes of advance.

We cannot allow present regional disparities to continue.

They will poison and embitter our whole national life. They will distort our economy and our society. There must be no timidity in our measures to eliminate them. This is a major aspect of our fight against injustice.

Poverty is Preventable

Twenty-nine years ago Beveridge challenged society to attack 'want'. He termed it with disease, ignorance, squalor and idleness as one of the 'five giants on the road of reconstruction'. By the early 1950's it seemed that the challenge had been met. Seebohm Rowntree's third study showed a dramatic reduction in poverty in the York of 1950 compared with the York of 1936. The mood of self-congratulation engendered by this study, and by the first experiences of affluence is now, however, sometime dead. In its place we have a strongly reawakened, if so far rather ill-defined, concern.

The forces that lie at the root of poverty are deep-seated, complex and frequently interconnected. To be effective, a radical attack on poverty must reflect these complexities. There are no easy solutions, no painless formulae. Poverty is many-sided. Some poor people have jobs; some do not—either because they are old or disabled, or simply because they cannot find one. Many large families live in poverty, but many of the poor have no dependants. The poor do not only have low incomes; often their incomes are uncertain too. Their work, when they are lucky enough to have it, is usually unsatisfying. Frequently, they live in cramped housing in the less attractive quarters of towns and cities. They may struggle to feed and clothe their children, but the schools to which their children go are often in run-down buildings, with a rapid turnover of staff. On average, there are fewer doctors and dentists in the areas where the amount of sickness per head is greatest. In areas with inadequate housing, little commerce and struggling industry, the local authorities are usually impoverished—and poor local authorities cannot afford to provide adequate social services and have to struggle to provide the recreational and cultural facilities which their richer neighbours can easily afford.

This concern has in different ways affected both political parties. The last Labour Government made a number of most important changes in the interests of the poor. It changed the balance between family allowances and tax allowances. It adopted, in part, the proposals of the Plowden Report for priority areas in primary education. Its Urban Programme provided money for day nurseries and much else. It began to change the lot of some of the poor who live in institutions—particularly of the mentally handicapped. It reformed the National Assistance system. The aim was to provide extra help to some, within a framework of social services for all.

The Conservatives claim that their plans for housing and social security arise from concern about poverty. Unselective social services have, we are told by them, failed to give enough help to the poor. The remedy lies in concentrating help on those in most need. The social services should provide residual services for them. The more affluent should rely on the private sector.

These two very different responses by the political parties start from rather the same view of poverty. It is a view which was common in the 1960's. It can be called the 'pocket of poverty' approach. The poor are a small minority of ghetto dwellers and of people with special handicaps. Poverty is a series of small islands in a sea of affluence. The general growth of the economy will relieve a great deal of poverty. Special efforts can be limited to help in small areas at our major cities. Changes required in social security are quite limited ones—mainly to give more help to a minority in need.

The 'pocket of poverty' approach has obvious attractions for political parties. It does not present many problems of choice

in public expenditure or in taxation. The innovations required
—such as the urban programme—have an appeal to conscience
and yet are inexpensive. But events are making this approach
obsolete. Partly through the actions of the Conservative
Government the question of poverty is now linked with an
even wider question—the whole future role of the social services. Nor are we likely to be able to eradicate poverty, except
as part of wider policies for social equality.

Help for people whose incomes are below the Supplementary
Benefit scale still comes first in any policy for poverty. Similarly we need to give help to the poorest areas in our major
cities. But these measures will not be enough in any longer
perspective towards the end of this decade.

Our approach has been too limited. First we have underestimated the scale of poverty in Britain. The number of people
with incomes below the official poverty line—Supplementary
Benefit scale rates—was about 2 million at the end of the
1960's. But a much larger number of people—about a fifth of
the population—10.6 million people—have incomes which are
quite near the poverty line. They have little economic security
and a high and constant risk of sinking into poverty, even by
the restricted official definition. No policy for poverty, which
is adequate, can ignore this much larger group. Any policy
which runs down the social services and replaces them by a
mixture of private provision and means tested services for the
few, is always in grave danger of helping the very poor at the
expense of the not quite so poor.

There is a second failure. We have failed I think to take a
general view of how those with low incomes are affected by
the whole interacting complex of policies on social security
and unemployment. A policy for poverty can no longer be
blind to the close inter-relationship between the social security
and the tax system. The two systems have become interlocked.
We are simultaneously taxing people into poverty and devising schemes to lift them out again. The recent surge of unemployment has had disastrous consequences for less skilled

workers, disabled workers and those with personal handicaps. A main aim in the 1970's must be to make sure that tax and unemployment policies help people on low incomes to achieve independence and reasonable living standards. It is low paid workers, older workers, disabled and less skilled workers who make up the bulk of the longer-term unemployed—not the young highly paid and highly trained. Help to the poor in the 1970's will require general changes in our tax, social security and economic policies. Special very limited programmes, however well meaning, will not be enough.

There are still more ways in which our approach has been unimaginative. We have failed to see the connections between poverty and serious regional and class inequalities in health care, education, housing and employment opportunities. A policy for poverty in the 1970's must include measures to deal with these inequalities.

Finally we have failed to see the connections between poverty and life in institutions. In the coming decade we must do much more to help those of the poor who are in institutions—such as old people's homes and hospitals for the mentally ill and handicapped—to lead normal lives in the community. This is even more urgent because medicine is keeping people alive much further into old age, where the risk of poverty is greatest. Similarly people with severe handicaps now have the chance of a more normal life. But the chance created by medicine can only be taken if our community services are much improved. Numbers in institutions have been growing in recent years. Most of those involved are drawn from the same groups as those in poverty in the wider community.

A more buoyant and economic climate would help the poor, both directly and indirectly. It would improve their chances of employment and clear the way for increased spending on the social services. But growth in itself will not necessarily mean either greater equality or benefit for people who are not at work. A great danger of the coming decade is that a considerable number of people will be shut off into a private world of chronically low incomes, restricted educational opportunities and bad housing. These conditions and opportunities will be carried over from one generation to the next. We have already created one such world—that of the old—but that, although highly undesirable in itself, is not as self-perpetuating, from generation to generation, as poverty earlier in life.

Our main concern is not now with the extremes of malnutrition. Tawney before the war wrote movingly about them in his *Equality*. Our concern is more with the effects of economic insecurity on people. Some may be able to rise above all practical deprivations—bad housing, poor opportunities in education or inadequate incomes. But for most existence under such conditions produces burdens and anxieties which reduce their whole quality of life. A child from an over-crowded home who goes to a bad school and leaves without knowledge and qualifications has poor prospects for employment and income. He is also less a person than he might otherwise have been. Mothers in the poor areas of our cities may be inadequate because of bad diet and housing. The pensioner who has to go into a home because of the shortage of community services often loses some substantial part of himself. Poverty in terms of an absolute standard of subsistence may now be much less harsh than in the past. But its effect on the individual cannot be defined except in relation to the standards of life around him. Relative deprivation stunts the opportunity for self-development.

I turn now to examine the scale of poverty today as a first step towards suggesting remedies. The poor are usually defined in terms of Supplementary Benefit scale rates. They are people who have incomes to meet all needs, including rent, of less than £1.26 a day for a single person and £1.90 a day for a married couple. By this extremely stringent standard it is likely, to judge from the most recent estimate, that about 2 million people, including dependants, or about 3.4 per cent of the population are in poverty. The numbers had shown little change over the 1960's; the old make up the majority of people in poverty. Poverty is more widespread amongst elderly women and is fairly widespread amongst the very old of both sexes. Apart from the old, poverty is to be found among families. Very few single people or childless couples below retirement age are in poverty. The recent Report on Two Parent Families calculates that about 105,000 such families with 316,000 children were in poverty in 1970—a little over one per cent of all families. Poverty was particularly common among large families but was certainly not confined to them. 39% of families in poverty had only one child. The report of the Prices and Incomes Board on Low Pay suggested that fatherless families in which the mother went out to work were usually in poverty. Women's wages at about 50 per cent those of men's are inadequate means on which to support a family. In general poverty is a problem of old age and of families where the head, often the mother, is in full-time work, but with very inadequate pay. The increase in family allowances in 1968 somewhat reduced family poverty, and FIS also helps very marginally, but family poverty remains a most serious problem.

A policy for poverty must also take account of those who are not necessarily currently in poverty, but are at risk. Obviously those receiving Supplementary Benefit would be in poverty without it. About 4.6 million people—including dependants—rely on such benefit. Most of these are women. About 1.8 million women were getting regular weekly payments in November 1971 compared to 1.1 million men. Among both sexes the elderly are more likely to be drawing benefit. About 65 per cent of the payments made are for Supplementary Pensions. The rest are made to the sick, the disabled, fatherless families and to the unemployed.

At least a further four million people have incomes which are only just above the Supplementary Benefit scale level. About 1.4 million pensioners have resources which are barely above. About 10 per cent of two parent families—2.6 million people —have net resources of less than £5 a week above the scale level. There are also some sick or unemployed who may not be drawing Supplementary Benefit but whose income is only a little above it. Thus the total of all those whose income is below, at or a little above Supplementary Benefit scale level is about 10.6 million—2 million below, 4.6 million on benefit and 4 million just above.

Poverty is not simply a question of having little money to spend. The poor are deprived in terms of health care, housing, education, and jobs. Not every poor person will suffer each and every one of these disadvantages. But most will experience one or more. Part of the punishment of being poor is to have bad health, and lower life expectancy. Class differences in opportunities for life and health start at the cradle and continue throughout life. The most recent survey of infant mortality in 1964-5 suggests that there is at least a 50 per cent greater chance that a baby from an unskilled or semi-skilled manual background will die in the first year of life than a baby whose father is a professional or white-collar worker. Children from these backgrounds will be smaller at school age. When they grow up and enter employment they are likely to have more and longer spells of sickness—as well as less favourable fringe benefits. The most recent detailed survey of sickness absence—carried out in 1961-2—showed that 28 per cent of all men recorded at least one period of incapacity in the year— but the proportion varied from 18 per cent for white collar workers to 35 per cent for unskilled workers. The average period of absence was 4.4 days for white-collar workers and 13.6 days for the unskilled. Unskilled workers have fewer natural teeth than white-collar and professional workers. They are more prone to bronchitis. The incidence of mental illness and of admission to mental hospitals is much higher among unskilled workers. The conclusion of Cooper writing in the British Journal of Social and Preventive Medicine for 1961 was that 'conditions of socio-economic stress suffered most by those in the lower social classes are important in the genesis of schizophrenia'. Class differences persist even at death. A recent study of Exeter showed that death rates both for men and women were significantly higher in the ward which had the highest proportion of unskilled workers.

Health standards differ between classes: they also differ between regions. Babies are healthier in the Home Counties than in Leeds and the rate of sickness absence for adults is lower in the South East than in Yorkshire.

Housing standards affect attitudes and the ability of children to learn. It is difficult to perform effectively outside if the home circumstances are those of over-crowding or damp. Poor housing standards reduce privacy, and make for difficulties in family life. Such standards are still common. The most recent evidence is that of the 1966 Census and of the 1967 housing survey. It suggests that 3 million dwellings had no inside lavatory and 2 million no fixed bath. More than a million people were living in conditions of severe over-crowding. The position has improved since 1966, but by no means for all. Dampness and decay contribute to an atmosphere of dereliction. The worst conditions are to be found in the North West, Yorkshire, and the London area. The financial position of many tenants in old housing is also unfavourable. The NBPI's Report on Low Pay showed paradoxically that the poorest families had the highest housing costs. The net weekly housing cost for all workers in the survey was then £2.10—but for the poorest it was £4.10. This is primarily because in cities families are more likely to live in private rented accommodation. They are unable to become owner-occupiers and achieve the resultant benefits of capital gains and tax relief. It was suggested by the Cullingworth Report that many local authorities discriminate against poorer families among potential tenants. Poor families are forced into the private rented sector with its high rents and low security of tenure.

Poor educational opportunities help to transmit poverty on from one generation to the next. The state of education reflects wide differences in access to higher education. In 1968 2 per cent of 18 year olds from unskilled manual backgrounds went to university compared to 35 per cent of 18 year olds from professional and managerial backgrounds. Children in the North leave school earlier. 63 per cent stayed on after 15 in the South East in 1969 compared to 47 per cent in the North. Educational Reports have looked at poverty in terms of the standards of schools. The Newsom Report's Survey published in 1963 of inner city secondary modern schools showed that the reading age of children in such schools was 17 months lower than in the average secondary modern school. The position may have improved somewhat since, but the gap has not been closed. In primary schools some children may be handicapped from early days by poverty of language and culture. The Plowden Report described forcefully the difficulties of primary schools in poor areas, arising from old buildings and bad staffing.

Finally poverty is a matter of employment prospects. Regional differences in opportunities are notorious. Less visible is the countrywide predicament of the unskilled. The general unemployment rate is not a good guide to their employment prospects. It reflects the experience of higher skill levels which even now run smaller risks of unemployment. The specific unemployment rate for the unskilled nationally is at least 10 per cent—and the position is even more serious for unskilled workers outside the South East and Midlands. A fall in the general level of unemployment would alleviate but not eliminate the problem. The longer-term prospects of a school leaver who has no qualifications and is not able to acquire training would remain bleak. He is likely to have both a low income over his working life and little security in employment.

Lack of skill blights the employment prospects of people in deprived areas. In the St. Anne's district of Nottingham, in parts of Central Liverpool and of Central Glasgow, to take three surveyed examples, there are particularly high concentrations of unskilled workers. They have earnings which are both low and spasmodic. They have higher rates of sickness and unemployment. They are trapped by poor standards of health, housing, education and jobs.

There is not one single simple remedy for poverty. But it could be massively attacked if we carry through certain policies. It is to these that I now turn. *Substantial spending will be required.* Finance will probably limit the speed at which the programme can be carried out. But sensible and realistic commitments will only follow from a view of longer-term objectives. It is vital to sort out these objectives. The first priority is that of short-term changes in social security benefits to help the 2 million people who are living below Supplementary Benefit level. But we also need changes in our tax and social security systems to improve the economic security of all that fifth of the population who are near the poverty level. Such changes in social security and taxation need to be accompanied by measures to help the less skilled to earn a living. But increased retraining would also be useful. The measures proposed, so far, would both raise the current incomes of these of the poor who cannot work, and raise the earning power of those who can. But we should also increase investment in the next generation. We must break the cycle by which the children of the poor become poor themselves. This will mean changes in our policies for the social services. Finally we need new efforts to provide alternatives to institutional care.

The aim of any scheme is to provide a reasonable minimum income for all. This was the Beveridge goal—but in practice no Government has yet achieved it. The state retirement pension has been below the Supplementary Benefit level. The National Insurance Pension for a married couple is now £10.90. Supplementary Benefit for a married couple, taking into account the rent allowance and the long term addition, is about £13.90. Nor has the level of family allowances reflected the subsistence costs of children. Currently the allowances are 90p or £1. The Supplementary Benefit scale allows £2.25 for a child aged five to eleven and more for an older child. The effect of the child tax allowances is to give more support to children from richer homes to those from poorer.

Various schemes have been proposed to provide a minimum

income for all. The boldest, simplest and quickest of these is the 'new Beveridge plan' combined with tax clawback. The increases in retirement pensions, family allowances and other National Insurance benefits needed to bring them to minimum subsistence levels would be very substantial.

The present Government has tried to deal with the problem by introducing the Family Income Supplement. Its disadvantages are great. The rate of take-up is low and is likely to remain so. It gives help only to those in the most dire need—and admittedly not even to all of them. Finally it adds one more to the great confusion of means tested benefits which face people on low incomes.

In the interests of incentives to hard work and initiative, the Government has reduced the maximum income tax and surtax liability, even on the highest incomes, to 75%. The top-paid will now therefore keep 25p on each further pound. Today the £21 a week man, however, will certainly take home less of each further pound *he* earns and may well actually take home *nothing* of an extra pound he has won by harder work or longer hours.

This absurdity arises simply because the Government, in order to make cuts in social expenditure—quite unnecessary in the present economic circumstances—have introduced a massive proliferation of means tests. Their housing and welfare measures will subject fully a third of the entire population to means tests. Altogether six or seven times more *working* families, that is with the man in full-time employment, will be liable to means tests than were subject previously to all other means tests put together—and there are 3,000 of them in Britain today.

Now all these means tests have a ceiling for eligibility within the same broad range of income. To the extent therefore that more and more means-tested benefits are concentrated on low wage earners, they will stand to lose more and more as they push up their earnings to, and beyond, this ceiling band. Consider the man on £21 a week with two children in July

1972. If he were able to push up his gross earnings, he would lose out of an extra pound:

	£
Income tax	.30
Loss of FIS	.10
Graduated contribution	.4
School meals charges	1.20
Rent allowance	.17
	£1.81

He is thus left 81p *worse off* as a result of his harder work, higher productivity or whatever. And there is nothing whatsoever exceptional about such a man.

If the family were also getting school uniform grants, education maintenance allowances, students' grants, family planning facilities and exemption from charges for prescriptions, spectacles and dental care, and for local authority services like home help and the care of the children (or any combination of these), the position would be still worse. Indeed recent research surveys have come across wage-earners subject to a disincentive of more than 200%; that is they would be more than twice as worse off for each extra £1 they earned.

This ridiculous situation, symbolised by the nonsense that a low wage-earner family may well be receiving FIS while at the same time paying income tax, is full of ironies. Labour has always feared the disincentive effects of accumulated means tests. Previously however when means tests were few and uncoordinated, such fears may have been insubstantial.

The Tories on the other hand have traditionally been suspicious about scrounging and evasion by the poor. Their fears have been grossly exaggerated, but now a Conservative Government have produced a situation in which incentive has been completely destroyed—and indeed reversed—for a very large segment of the population.

The other possible approaches are those of negative income tax or of tax credit schemes. In principle, these schemes have strong intellectual appeal and certainly deserve more careful and detailed consideration than they have received so far. Some versions of the schemes are open to the objection that they give help only to the few; all of them pose very considerable administrative problems, although over a period these should not be insurmountable.

In any case the tax and social security systems have to be brought closer together. In 1968 I took the first step in this direction when I raised family allowances substantially by combining the increase with a tax clawback provision. We must now move towards a complete integration of child tax allowances and family allowances. Instead of these two forms of payment, families would receive a child endowment payment which would be partly taxable—and they would receive this payment for all children including the first.

Changes in social benefits are clearly necessary in the attack on poverty. These involve considerable financing problems, which are far more easily solved within a generally buoyant economy climate. Such changes are not imperative if we are to help the 2 million in poverty. Where they are needed is to help the other 9 million who are near the poverty line. The current faults in our social security and tax systems are felt most severely at these levels of income. The first fault is that we lack an adequate pension scheme. It was a major tragedy that we just failed to leave one on the Statute Book at the end of the last Labour Government. Occupational pensions schemes have grown rapidly because the state has not provided a decent alternative. The old pension scheme has even failed in its relatively limited objective of providing minimum for all. The better off have occupational pensions. It is the poor who have suffered.

It must be accepted that the tax system is very hard on

poorer families because the tax threshold is so low. I raised it several times but not as much as I would have liked or as was necessary. It is now relatively much lower than 20 years ago. In 1950 a married man with one child started paying tax when his earnings reached 75 per cent of the national average. Now he starts paying tax when his earnings are a little over half the average. This means that a family can both pay tax and receive benefit under the Family Income Supplement. A family with one child and an income of £19.50 a week gross will get a payment of 30p under FIS—but will pay almost the same amount in tax. We have moved away from the old principle that we should not tax the income required for subsistence.

We must also recognise that our social services are no longer on a par with the best. Our system of family support is less generous or equitable than in most European countries. Our post-war pension scheme has also worn less well than the American social security system. The view is taking hold that the social services should act as a safety net to private provision. Yet only the state—as the American experience shows—can run an adequate pension service. The firm—in a time of rapid change in labour markets and in the structure of industry—is the wrong unit on which to base provision for old age. Who can predict the structure of industry in thirty years time? Nor can pension arrangements based on firms do much for those who work outside the more prosperous and capital intensive sectors of industry. Equally only government can bring about redistribution in favour of families.

Changes in social security are the first part of any programme for poverty. The second is help to the less skilled in the job market. Job prospects matter to all the high risk groups which make up the poor. They matter to the elderly, to single parent families, to large families and to unskilled workers. Some pensioners are in full or part time employment, as are some single women supporting families. Job prospects affect every group among the poor—not simply the adult male wage earning poor.

Unemployment at its 1966-70 level—let alone today's far worse level—is damaging to the vulnerable groups in the labour force. A return to full employment would substantially brighten the job prospects of the unskilled. It would also reduce the numbers of disabled drawing Supplementary Benefit. Some of them would be able to find jobs in a more buoyant labour market. Fuller employment would help not only the very poor but that fifth of the population whose standard of living is constantly under threat. We have to create economic conditions such that the chance of a job and of self-respect is open to older workers and the less skilled—not just to the young and the highly trained.

We must also change our policies for the other social services, such as education. The standard of schools in poor areas is too low. Hence special help has been given to Plowden priority areas. But the problem may not just be that schools in a few areas are inadequate. There may have been a wider shift of emphasis within our social services.

Originally the purpose of the social services was to relieve poverty. So great was the need that almost any increase in public spending in whatever form helped to reduce poverty. This is no longer the case. The social services have come to serve many accepted social purposes other than the relief of poverty. They provide opportunities in higher education. They attempt to achieve a reasonable pattern of urban development, through the new towns policies. They provide care in sickness for all. This is in itself very desirable. It is essential for a civilised life. But it also means an increase in the general level of public spending may not in itself reduce poverty. It all depends on who gets the increase.

Some of the fastest growth in spending recently has been for services from which the poor benefit little. Few children from an unskilled manual background go to university. Few of the poor move into new housing in new towns.

We must be careful that services which are used by the less affluent get their full share of extra resources. We must be concerned with the distribution of the services as well as their scale. We must, within the framework of a high standard of universal services, direct more help to poorer areas and groups. There may be a case for priority areas in the NHS as well as in education and in housing. We have greatly underestimated the human and financial resources required to improve standards in deprived areas.

There is one further change in our policies for the social services which would be of great help to the poor. This would be an increased commitment to the personal social services, for children needing help and guidance in the schools, for the disabled and for the old. The extension and development of community care has a particular importance for groups at risk of poverty. This is so for children in deprived families. In the schools there is a grave shortage of psychologists, psychiatrists and trained staff concerned with child guidance. The Seebohm Report calculated that at least one child in ten will need special educational, social or mental help before the age of 18 and that at most one child in twenty-two was getting such help. In parts of the country children in distress may have to wait many months for an appointment. Children with educational handicaps suffer as well as those with physical and emotional difficulties. Disturbed adolescents also get little help. Troubles in school contribute to employment problems later. A child whose school career is interrupted or hampered will often leave without qualifications and will find it difficult to get and keep a job. Help earlier might make the difference between poverty and the ability to earn an adequate living later.

The elderly also need personal services. They use meals on wheels, home nursing, the home help and chiropody services. Better services are need as well as improved pensions if we are to eliminate poverty in old age. In most local authority areas these services are quite inadequate. We need much more sheltered housing and more help so that the elderly can continue to lead a normal life in the community. Even at present the great majority of the bed-bound and the house-bound live at home and not in institutions. We need to develop both services which help the infirm among the elderly and those which help the elderly to maintain their independence.

Finally a policy for poverty must involve help to those in institutions. The poor are much more likely than the population as a whole to find themselves at some stage in life in institutions, whether these are homes for the elderly, psychiatric hospitals or even prisons. The elderly poor are often in local authority residential accommodation. People from unskilled occupations are more frequently admitted to mental hospitals. Hospitals for the handicapped have a number of patients who could lead a fairly normal life in the community if they were helped to do so.

The institutional populations are growing rather than shrinking. At present about 320,000 people are in institutions—counting only local authority old people's homes, and hospitals for the mentally ill and handicapped. For one group—children in care, there have been significant advances away from institutional care. But we have not moved nearly as rapidly to provide a more normal life for other groups.

These institutions have common effects on the personality. They lead to the destruction of identity and the reduction of independence. In spite of the efforts of staff, most of our institutions in their present form make people worse not better. Progress here will be slow, but we can and must do better than we have done in the last decade. In the past we have adopted the slogans of community care, without always making the practical commitments. We have had plans for community care—for instance that for the mentally ill. But we have not in practice carried them nearly far enough.

Social, health and education services tend to be provided at a lower level relative to need in the areas where the need is greatest. This is not usually the fault of the local authorities.

At root, it is the fault of the system within which they have to operate.

Local authority expenditure is paid for partly out of rates and partly—58%—out of Rate Support Grant from the Government. Poor areas suffer a multiple handicap; the yield of a 1p rate per head of the population is low, poor people can ill afford high rates, yet the formula which redistributes Rate Support Grant does not take fully into account the effects of variations in resources and the costs of providing services. I have already stressed the need for additional sources of revenue for local authorities; but we must reform the existing rating system as well. At present the ordinary householder's rate bill is determined less by conscious political decisions of his elected representatives than by the quirks of the Rate Support formula and by the accident of whether his home is within the same local authority boundaries as a reasonable spread of factories, shops and offices. If Central Government is to cede to local authorities control over a substantial source of revenue—be it local income tax or one of the major indirect taxes—then I believe rates from industry and commerce should be redistributed directly by the Government to local authorities on a basis of need.

This would end the present situation, where the authorities which can afford the highest level of expenditure per person are simply those with a substantial rate yield from commercial and industrial property. The wealth of Westminster, Croydon and even Port Talbot would go to improve facilities in less fortunate areas. This would be an important change, for the demands on local authority expenditure created by industry and commerce are in no way proportional to the income which they provide to the local authority under today's system. We often find that the authority where industry and commerce are situated is not the authority where the people who work in the factories and shops and offices are living. And it is people, particularly the young and the old, on whose behalf most local authority expenditure is incurred. However, if a local authority did not derive any immediate financial benefit from additional commerce and industry, there would be less pressure to build offices and shops where it should be building homes and health centres and libraries.

Redistribution of the Rate Support Grant goes a long way to help the poor authority, but it does not overcome the whole of its handicap. If an authority wishes to improve or extend its services, it can do so by raising its rates. This is a straightforward choice for the richer areas which are the least likely to have a great need to compensate by unusually high standards of public provision for unusually low standards of amenity for the people who live there. It is the poor authority which most needs a generous supply of school books and equipment, or of social workers, or a well-staffed and equipped children's service. But the people who live in these areas are least able to pay higher rates. They can best be helped by a continuing positive redirection of resources, over and above the redistribution of grant according to needs.

To do this we need an expanded Urban Programme not only for the renewal and redevelopment of outmoded or unsuitable buildings or other capital stock, but also to give continuing support to welfare and community development projects, some of which are voluntary as well as to improve the standard of the ongoing services which the local authority provides. The present scale of the Urban Programme is very small. Local authority current expenditure totals some £4,000 million a year; local authority capital expenditure is another £2,000 million. Yet expenditure on the Urban Programme, to direct additional resources where they are most needed, is estimated to rise to a grand total of little over £14 millions in 1972/3. There is no shortage of worthy projects. In 1971, for example, the London Borough of Lambeth submitted projects to cost £103,500. Only £13,650 of this was approved for inclusion in the Urban Programme. An eightfold expansion of the whole programme would cost only about £120 million per year. This is not too heavy a price to pay to attack the manifold squalor in areas where poverty abounds.

It is for Government to ensure that public standards of provision are *higher* in relation to needs in areas where there is poverty than they are elsewhere. To make them equally high would be a good start, but it is only by positive discrimination that we can hope to break into the vicious circle of poverty and deprivation that we see about us.

I have endeavoured to outline the problem and suggest some but not complete remedies. We will achieve little until we make the reduction of poverty a goal of our general social and economic policies. Poverty can be eliminated only if we improve the standards of our social services generally, and change our priorities for them. Poverty can only be eliminated if we make it a goal of our general economic policies and make a success of those policies.

The main danger is that our society will become increasingly divided between the affluent and the less well off. On one side will be the world of youth and opportunities—on the other the poor, with an increasing sense of deprivation and shut-offness from the affluent world about them. The old are still far too much in a deprived world on their own. Let us make sure that we do not allow to persist still longer another private world of continuing hopelessness for at least a fifth of our citizens. That would be the road to a dangerously split, morally unjust and damagingly insecure society of which none of us could be proud.

The Developing World

Of all the forms of injustice which disfigure the world today, injustice between the rich and poor nations, a blatant and growing chasm between the levels of existence—at the lower end of the scale they can hardly be graced with the label 'standard of living'—is the most dangerous for the whole future of civilization upon this planet. It is not something to which we can or should shut our eyes. At least 500 million people in the world will not have had enough to eat today. The countries they live in may have produced some moderate overall economic growth. They may have given themselves a thin, developed veneer—a few hotels and a modern airport in the main city. More importantly there may have been some real progress in education and health. But 500 million people are still just about as hungry as their forebears—they were fewer then—were ten or twenty or fifty or a hundred years ago.

It is a killing hunger. One in three of the children in Asia and Africa die before they grow up. And many of those who live are made stupid for life by the damage that hunger has done to their brain cells. And that happens in a world that spends twenty years' worth of aid to get to the moon, where most people in rich countries are overweight through eating too much, where we would be horrified at not providing proper food for British or American cats and dogs.

And we do little enough to make it better. The share of its income that the West gives as aid has fallen every year since 1961. And quite often a lot of the aid that is given is not much real help to poor people in poor countries. Quite often it gets lost on the way down. Quite often it is more of a help to our less efficient exporters than to the recipients. And quite often too we frustrate its purposes by restrictive trade policies, which turn the poor countries in upon themselves, and leave them to try to cope with the masses of jobless, propertyless, hungry and desperate people who are bound to be a ready target for propaganda from the advocates of violence and disruption. It is remarkable not that some régimes falter in their democratic commitment, but the extent to which, most notably in India, freedom and representative government have survived against these appalling hindrances.

We cannot contract out of these problems. If there is one continuous thread which most unites those who stand on the Left in politics it is our belief that most problems are community problems, that we all share a responsibility for what happens around us, that there can be no worthwhile life based on an indifference to everyone else. And if no man can be an island, no country can be either. To try to shut oneself off is not only a selfish but an ineffective approach. The world will not go away. On the contrary, every modern development, whether beneficial or harmful, brings it crowding in more closely upon us.

The future prospects of human security and satisfaction depend upon benefits being more widely spread. In the Labour Party we believe this without question in relation to this country. We reject utterly a future in which one man's prosperity, one area's prosperity, is based upon the degradation of another. It is equally true in the wider world. We cannot believe in a socialism which stops either at Land's End or John O'Groats. Even if—and it is a very big if—we could solve all our domestic problems on our own, there would be little inspiration or even security in a cellophane-wrapped Britain, hoping like a Western tourist in an Inter-Continental hotel that he was safe both from infection and the upheaval of the land around him.

As the remaining decades of this century unfold, as the world gets smaller and as the balance of population shifts more and more towards the developing countries, we will all of us in the West, however well we order our own affairs, be in increasing danger of living like those in the grand apartment houses of Upper Manhattan, looking across with a mixture of fear and incomprehension at the festering ghettos of Harlem. Our belief in the universality of human rights should unite with an enlightened self-interest to make us reject such a future. Only if there is rapid progress towards a fairer world can we ensure that the receding tensions of East-West relations are not replaced by a still more dangerous and deep-seated cleavage between the rich and the poor world. 700 million people—a third of the two billion people living in the developing world—live in the Indian sub-continent. In India itself 40% of the population—200 million people—live on less than 5 pence a day. Calcutta is the most frightening human agglomeration in the world. Nine million people live there, most of them in conditions of unimaginable poverty, conditions as degrading as they are insanitary. And Calcutta as a city was entirely a British creation. To-day, its problems make even those of Bangladesh seem containable. We cannot shrug off responsibility for such a degree of human suffering.

It is against this background that we should consider what has been achieved, and how much more needs to be done. At UNCTAD in the Spring of 1972 Robert McNamara, President of the World Bank, said bluntly that 'the state of development in most of the developing world today is unacceptable—and growing more so'. It is true that the overall target for the 'sixties—the first United Nations Development Decade—was met, although 90% of the investment finance came from the poor countries themselves, only 10% from aid, and none at all from private investment, which was all balanced by profits sent back to rich countries. An average annual increase of 5% in national income was achieved. But it is not sufficient to set an overall target rate of growth for all developing countries. Just as we in this country would not be satisfied by meeting a 5% growth target by 8% in the South-east and 2% growth in Scotland, so we as members of the international community cannot be satisfied when, among the less developed countries, the relatively rich oil-exporting countries, with less than 4% of the population, grow at 8.4% per year, whilst the poorest countries, with 67% of the population and with average incomes per head of less than £80 per year, grow at less than half that rate. Moreover, income per head in these poorest countries grew at only 1.5% each year.

While the gap between the rich and the poor worlds has stubbornly failed to narrow, the gap between the rich and the poor within many developing countries has widened. In Brazil in 1960, the poorest 40% of the population received only 10% of the national income. By 1970 their share had fallen to 8%. Meanwhile, the richest 5% had increased their share from just under 30% to almost 40%. Much the same happened in Mexico. Latin America provides the most flagrant examples of inequality between rich and poor, but even outside Latin America most developing countries suffer inequalities far more stark than any we have known in Britain in living memory. In Britain today, about 30% of the national income goes to the richest 10% of the population. That is bad enough; but in the developing world 30% of the national income goes on average to the richest 5%. By a cruel paradox, moreover, the so-called Green Revolution in agriculture—which has made it possible to double wheat production, for example, in the areas where new techniques have been introduced—has benefitted mainly the wealthy farmers, who are sophisticated enough and have large enough holdings of land to apply the new methods properly. The poor are almost as hungry as ever. In Asia and Latin America food production per head was no greater in 1971 than in 1958: in Africa it was smaller.

And the hunger of the poor feeds on itself. Malnutrition, above all protein malnutrition, can permanently retard mental and physical capacity. It also leads to appallingly high rates of infant mortality. In the developing world, children under five account for one-fifth of the population, but for three-fifths of the deaths. High rates of infant mortality lead in turn to high birth rates, for when many children die in infancy, large families provide the only insurance that some children will survive. Yet it has become increasingly clear in the last ten years that the world's population cannot go on growing indefinitely at its present rate without intolerable results. At the fall of the Roman empire, mankind numbered about 400 million. By 1600 the figure had grown to 1,000 million. By 1900 it was 2,000 million. Today, world population is about 3,700 million. If present trends continue, it will reach about 6,700 million by the year 2000, and it will still be growing.

Almost all the growth will have taken place in the poorer parts of the world. Food production would have to expand enormously to keep the extra millions alive. Such an expansion may be technically feasible. Even so, the ecological costs would certainly be high and might be prohibitive. But this is not a reason for despair. In the developed world, birth rates used to be much higher than they are today. They fell as living standards rose—partly because contraceptive techniques improved, but much more because the rates of child mortality were reduced, because education spread, because state provision for the elderly improved, and because as a result of all this, parents decided that they wanted smaller families. In the long run, similar advances in the developing world will produce similar results. But there is little time to spare. The lesson of history is that the key to lower birth rates lies in a fall in the desired family size—and that key can be turned only by increased prosperity. It is vitally important, not only for the developing countries themselves, but for the rest of us as well, that their population policies should succeed, and succeed quickly. But it is idle to expect success unless their economies expand more rapidly than they have done until now—and unless the benefits of growth are channelled firmly in the direction of the poor.

We must do much more than we have done so far to close the gap between the rich and poor countries. Above all, we must do much more to close the gap between the rich and poor inside the developing countries. How can this be done?

We have learned much in the last ten years. We have learned that the path to increasing prosperity does not lie in a slavish imitation of the Western model—or of the Soviet model either. In the developed world economic growth has been associated with advances in capital-intensive technology. The more we can install machines to do the work of men the faster labour productivity will grow and the more prosperous we shall become. Even in the developed world such attitudes now have a hollow ring. In developing countries they can be a fatal blind alley, however attractive they may be to governments understandably anxious to rescue their peoples from colonial exploitation. In most developing countries primary products comprise a high proportion of exports, most people earn their living from the land, and labour is abundant while jobs are scarce. In such economies, the emphasis must be not on saving labour but on using it, not on increasing output per man but on creating jobs for men to do. New agricultural techniques are needed, yes—but they must be labour-intensive techniques. Increasingly, agricultural and other products should be processed before they are exported—but again, by labour-intensive methods. And new labour-intensive industries must be developed, for it is only by increasing employment outside the agricultural sector that the benefits of industrial growth can be distributed beyond a small enclave of the privileged.

We have learned that it is at least as important to improve agriculture as it is to develop industry. In the developing world at least 70% of the population depends on farming for its meagre living. A quarter of the exports of developing countries are of agricultural products. Yet only one-fifth of government investment in education and health goes to agricultural areas. Less than 12% of foreign aid goes to agriculture, and much of that goes to the bigger farmers. In Africa and Latin America, the proportion of the contribution which agriculture makes to the national income which is then spent on agricultural research is less than one-tenth of what it is in most rich countries. Yet the returns to such research can be immense. The agricultural revolution of the past decade has so far affected only wheat, rice and maize. The new agriculture requires irrigation—but more than three-quarters of India's arable land, and about half of Pakistan's has no irrigation. Research on other crops and on varieties which can be grown without irrigation is an urgent need. The immediate ecological fears about the Green Revolution have been exaggerated: to-day the whole of Asia uses only one-tenth as much fertilizer per head as Europe does, while the United States uses even more than Europe. It is in the rich world that we need to worry most about damaging the soil and the environment.

Above all we have learned how urgent is the need for more aid from outside. The average income per head in this country is now about £750 per year. The average income of the 75% of the world who live in less developed countries is about £70 a year. During the 'seventies—the Second Development Decade—the projected increase for the 25% who live in rich countries is nearly £500 a head. For the others, it is £40. And this presupposes that flows of official aid are raised to meet the target of 0.7% of Gross Domestic Product. To do this will cost the developed world 1½% of its likely £500 per head *increase* in average income, leaving the other 98½% to be enjoyed at home. It is hardly an excessive price to try to make it possible for those on £70 a year to get an extra £40. Yet Britain has not even accepted the target.

Britain's official aid last year was 0.38% of GDP By 1975 it is planned to rise to 0.43%. But by then Australia, Belgium, Canada, Denmark, France and the Netherlands—all already ahead of us—plan to reach 0.60% Norway and Sweden plan to pass the United Nations target of 0.70% and two other European countries will be very near to it.

Britain is unlike nearly all the other donor countries in

refusing to accept this target. It prefers the old UNCTAD target of 1% of GNP for all financial flows to developing countries. The reason for this preference is simple but not acceptable. We have a fairly heavy outward flow of private investment capital. In both 1969 and 1970 total flows from Britain to developing countries exceeded 1%. So, in fact, did flows from five other countries. But private investment overseas is not an adequate substitute for official aid. Private investment goes where the prospect of short- or medium-term profit is highest. Private investment goes where companies, especially multi-national companies, see opportunities for maximizing their own profit rather than the benefit to the country in which they invest. There is nothing wrong in this, but no government should pretend that it is providing aid in the form most helpful to the developing countries when it is simply encouraging private investors to maximize their own profits by investing overseas.

Now that we are no longer pinned down by perennial balance of payments difficulties, we should not be less forthcoming than our fellow members of the OECD Development Assistance Committee. Indeed, we should go further. We should take the lead in trying to reach international agreement to raise the target for official aid to 1.0% of GDP by the end of the Second Development Decade.

Yet even official aid is not always what it seems. Some aid takes the form of loans at rates of interest not much lower than would be available commercially. But because of interest rates on past loans, some countries carry a huge burden of debt; much of the aid they receive today is used to provide the foreign exchange to finance this. In India, debt re-payments pre-empt about 20% of export earnings, in Indonesia about 25%, and in Pakistan nearly 30%. In 1970, the Soviet Union, Japan, and Italy all received more in debt repayments from India than they disbursed as aid. This is souring India's whole attitude to aid. Britain very seldom receives a net inflow from any of its aid programmes, but none the less, past lending was

C

often on much 'harder' terms than current aid. We should put repayment of past loans to us on to easier terms, and we should try to reach agreement with other donors together to reduce the repayments of vast official debts. Some of the poorest countries in the world would gain greatly from such a change of policy.

Much aid is tied. Some of it is double-tied—it is tied to a specific project, and goods for that project have to be procured from the lender country. The value of gross aid flows has to be adjusted downwards by at least 10%, and sometimes by as much as 20% or even 50%, to allow for the effect of these conditions in reducing the benefit derived from the aid, compared with an untied grant.

Such practices offer obvious short-term advantages to the donor country. The higher the interest charges, the less the cost of the aid. The more its aid is tied, the larger the guaranteed market for its own exports. If the aid were not tied, the developing country would buy where its needs were met most effectively and most cheaply. Tying gives the donor a protected market for its own inefficient producers and can thus postpone unpleasant change. Tying enables it to export the type of goods, often those suited to a capital-intensive technology, which it can most easily produce.

Aid which is fully aid is in the form of grants, not loans. Australia, Norway and Denmark provided over 90% of their aid commitments in the form of grants in 1970; Sweden and Switzerland over 80%; Britain provided only 50%. Aid without procurement tying enables the developing country to choose the most suitable supplier. But 64% of Britain's bilateral aid in 1970 was procurement tied.

The British aid doctrine used to be that aid should be given only to cover the foreign currency components of a particular project. This was particularly unhelpful. The doctrine has now been softened slightly so that some proportion of 'local costs' can sometimes be included. But this is still not good enough. There is a bias towards using aid for unnecessary imports unless it is given in the form of a general grant for a project or programme. If grants are made towards all costs, then no type of programme, however low its direct import content, is excluded from consideration for aid. The developing country can choose what helps it most. Too often in the past, aid has been available for grandiose visible projects: for, say, the construction of an air-conditioned airport with labour-saving luggage loaders, yet not for a widespread programme of minor irrigation works which would provide a far greater benefit to the developing country.

Whether aid is given bilaterally, or multi-laterally through an international agency, there is a tremendous problem in deciding how to allocate it. Developing countries almost inevitably resent detailed interference, however well-meaning, by donor countries in their own affairs. Yet donors need to appraise the use to which their aid is put if they are to act responsibly in allocating it. Only where there is complete confidence in the intentions of the developing country and its ability to carry them out can aid be given in the form of general budgetary support, though this is obviously the method which recipients prefer, since it leaves them free to organize their own developments.

Increasing internal inequalities, especially in Latin America, pose a difficult problem for donors who want to ensure that their aid is used to help the poorest. It would be wrong to discriminate against some of the very poor simply because they live in countries where we think the régime is far from perfect—but where we have doubts about the intentions or abilities of the government to channel aid so to diminish internal inequalities, we must seek acceptable methods of ensuring that our aid is used for the direct relief of poverty. Sweden has told developing countries that she is prepared to support programmes only if they can be shown to bring benefits to the really poor. We should follow this example; a much higher proportion of our aid should be directed towards agriculture, social programmes, population control and technical assistance to rural areas.

It is not sensible to allocate significant amounts of aid to those amongst the developing countries which are relatively rich. There is pressure from business interests to expand our bilateral aid to Latin America, where less than 10% of Britain's bilateral aid goes at present. This pressure must be resisted; Latin American countries in general are less poor than developing countries in Asia and Africa, and their governments are in general far less willing to ensure that the aid is distributed to benefit the poor sections of the community. By every criterion, countries in Asia and Africa are countries where the need is far greater. Total aid receipts each year from 1968-70 were less than $2 per head in India, Burma, Nigeria, Egypt and the Sudan. Pakistan and Indonesia received less than $4 per head—whilst the relatively rich Dutch Antilles received more aid per head of the population than the whole income of the average Indian. British aid in this period was split almost evenly between Asia and Africa—but whilst about 800 million people live in India, Pakistan, Bangladesh and Indonesia alone, scarcely more than a third as many live in the whole of Africa. These huge Asian countries are as poor as most of Africa; there is every reason to direct a higher proportion of British aid towards them. There is no good argument at all that any significant proportion of British bilateral aid should be directed anywhere other than to the two needy continents of Asia and Africa.

But there is every reason why most of the expansion of British aid, and of world aid, should not be bilateral, but multilateral. The World Bank is now using soft loans to help projects which reduce inequality and increase employment. We should help to provide an automatic source of funds for this work, so that the multilateral agencies become less vulnerable to the quirks of political fortune in the rich countries. A link with the creation of Special Drawing Rights by the International Monetary Fund is important. The most promising suggestion is that when the IMF creates extra reserves in the form of Special Drawing Rights and distributes them among its member countries in proportion to their quotas, each developed country would forego a portion of its allocation, in proportion to its national income. The amounts foregone would go to the multilateral aid agencies, to be distributed to developing countries. Provided such an SDR link is viewed as a supplement to existing aid, it is by far the most promising way to ensure a relatively steady increase in world aid flows. If $1 billion—about £400 million—were provided annually through such a link the cost would be barely one two-thousandth part of the national product of the developed countries. But aid through multilateral agencies would be almost doubled. Total official aid would be increased by nearly 15%.

Aid is only one way to help developing countries. There is no advantage for anyone in providing aid which increases exports by the developing country if these cannot be sold for increased foreign exchange earnings.

The developing world encounters formidable trade difficulties. Partly they are the result of mistaken development policies in the past; poor countries were encouraged to produce import substitutes rather than exports. We know now it is much better for them to restrict imports less and to concentrate on exporting what they can best produce—provided they are allowed to sell it to the rich countries. The tariff and quota policies of the rich world are of crucial importance here. Obviously, poor countries cannot allow free entry to British or EEC exports—unless, in return, we lower our trade barriers to imports from these countries. It is because of US, British and European failures here that countries like India are so inward-looking—or increasingly concentrate their trade on the USSR.

At the second UNCTAD in 1968, the main goal of the poor countries was to persuade the rich countries jointly to adopt a generalized preference scheme. They failed, although Britain in fact supported them. Individual countries and trade blocs have introduced their own schemes. The most important of these is that of the EEC. This came into effect in the summer of 1971 and is to last for ten years. It sets tariff-free quotas for each product. The quotas are set so low that they allow a rate of growth of imports less than that at which imports from poor countries have been growing anyway. Such a scheme, if it were applied by all the rich countries, would be only a small improvement on the present situation. If all poor countries' exports were admitted duty-free, the gain could be at least three times as great—equivalent to about 12% of net aid flows to them in 1970. To deny this benefit to poor countries is miserly and also foolish.

There will be no conviction that rich countries have any deep commitment to helping poor countries while aid goes hand-in-hand with trade restrictions. It is not only that developed countries try to protect their own industries from competition from the developing world. They spend heavily on research to find substitutes for the goods which the developing countries could supply more cheaply, so that they keep out the goods of the developing countries without even protecting their own employment. Why do the strong protect themselves so much against the weak? The answer lies in inertia, selfishness and lack of imagination. It is easier to erect a tariff barrier and carry on as before than it is to adjust to meet a new situation. Dismantling a trade barrier brings benefits to the consumers who enjoy the new cheap imports; it is painful for the producers in the rich countries until they can adapt to producing other goods. There can be gains for all from a liberal trade policy, but only if there is an active regional and industrial policy to cushion the impact on the industries most affected whilst resources are directed elsewhere. If there is not, the gains will be sullied by the imposition of unjustified hardship upon some sections of the community in the developed countries.

Among the developed countries, Britain's record on trade

questions is relatively good. Many of the more outward-looking EEC political leaders have hoped that Britain will give a new direction to EEC trade policies. In August 1973 negotiations will begin again between the EEC and the developing countries which want association. These talks are part of the process of providing a replacement for the Yaoundé convention, which expires in January 1975. This gives trade preferences to certain countries, mainly in French-speaking Africa—but these are countries with only 4% of the population of the less developed world. We must ensure that other African countries receive equality of treatment with the Yaoundé countries and that Asian countries also receive much freer access for their exports.

Encouragement to process goods before exporting them is what developing countries need, but here the structure of the EEC preference system is totally unsatisfactory. The really important manufactured exports from poor countries—textiles and processed food—face very stiff EEC tariff barriers. There is substantial support from within the existing Community for the proposal of Sicco Mansholt, the President of the Brussels Commission, to UNCTAD last month, that as the restructuring of EEC agriculture progresses, the EEC should increase its imports of goods like sugar, cereals, fats and oils. Developing countries produce these more cheaply than Europe. Britain's preference scheme for these goods from poor countries is more liberal than the EEC scheme; we must make sure that we do not move in the direction of the EEC scheme, but make the EEC move towards us. Not only members of the EEC Commission but many ordinary people in Europe would like to enjoy the cheaper products that a more liberal trade policy would bring.

Britain must make sure that the EEC adopts outward-looking trade policies towards the developing world; it must also use its entry as an opportunity to improve EEC aid policy. Bilateral aid of course remains the concern of the individual countries; it is the EEC aid institutions which can be greatly strengthened by Britain's entry. In principle, these are excellent multilateral aid-giving institutions, although less than 10% of EEC aid is channelled through them. But very nearly all the aid which they disburse goes to the Yaoundé countries, as does most French bilateral aid. French bilateral aid is not our direct concern, but EEC aid will concern us, and it represents a gross misallocation of resources. Each year from 1968-70, the European Development Fund gave on average $10 million to Asia, and ten times as much to the franc area in Africa. This bias must be redressed.

The present Government shows no sign of taking any of these questions seriously. Yet if the developing world is neglected, it is only its problems which will grow. An economy with confidence in its own powers of adjustment to meet changing situations can act courageously to increase official aid, to increase the proportion of it which is multilateral and to liberalize trade. A frightened country turns in on itself, and tries to shut out the dangers of the outside world. The next few years are vital for the developing countries because of the appalling problems which they still face, even though growth has now become a real possibility. They are vital for our relationship with developing countries particularly because of the forthcoming negotiations within the EEC. This is our best opportunity to turn the EEC outwards away from French colonial links. It is our best opportunity to ensure that Europe, emerging as the most powerful trading bloc in the world, can assume a new leadership role by becoming an accepted force not only for European but for world progress.

Such a role becomes of increasing importance as the United States continues, as I fear it will, to offer less to the Third World. The greatest deficiency in the world aid scene at the present time is the poor performance of the world's richest country. In the early 'sixties she allocated 0.5% of her vast GNP to official aid. In 1971 that figure was down to 0.31% and by 1975 it is projected to fall to 0.24%. This is against a background of an expenditure of $128 billion—over £50,000 million—on the Vietnam War over the past seven years. This has been a tragic misdirection of effort. If even a half that amount could have been spent on developing the poor world, instead of raining ineffective bombs upon a tiny corner of it, we would have a very different picture today.

I speak as a friend and not as a natural critic of the United States. I deeply respect many aspects of American life. I believe that over most of the past thirty years the American contribution to the world has been unique and that we all owe an immense debt to her generosity and her leadership during this period. The tragedy of allowing this ill-fated and horrible involvement to tear the country apart at home and to undermine both the power and the acceptability of its leadership abroad, has been of epic proportions. That war has done enough damage already, damage extending far beyond the casualties on the soil of Vietnam, terrible though these have been. Surely experience now proves many times over that any military move exacerbates and not heals the wound to the United States. Surely it is now the duty of any friend and ally to beg Washington to learn from these abundant lessons and to extricate herself before further crippling damage is done to the whole future of the United States and the West.

But even if that is achieved we must expect that for the next decade America, having suffered this tragic and unnecessary defeat, will have somewhat less concern and energy for the rest of the world than has been the case for the past generations. That is the opposite of a reason for any lack of commitment on our part. It makes our role, and that of Europe as a whole, still more crucial. The question for us is whether, as the remaining decades of this century wear on, we shall find ourselves living anxiously on an insecure pinnacle of wealth, surrounded by a menacing and increasingly embittered majority of the world, or whether by imagination, generosity and understanding, we can develop and spread our wealth so as to feel proud of the world in which we live and of our part in it.

Europe Past and Future

Speech at Aachen on receiving the Charlemagne Prize
11th May 1972

The inspiration of this great award, by which you honour me today, extends back over nearly 1,200 years. But its actual history covers only 22 years. Yet those 22 most recent years are not merely the most vivid because they are those most of us have experienced. They are also in many ways the most constructive and rewarding of the whole history of Western Europe. They do not represent the period of Europe's greatest dominance. That came earlier, when Europe, and particularly the central and western parts of it, were in every sense the hub of the world, when Washington was first an unnamed swamp and then a remote and inward-looking capital, when Moscow was barely on the edge of civilization, and when most of what we now know as the Third World was *terra incognita*.

But although throughout these centuries Europe was supreme she was far from ordering her own affairs with a perfect authority. Aachen, as the traditional Imperial City and the meeting point of so many of the tributaries which make up the river of European civilization, was both a symbol of the attempts at unity and a heavy sufferer when Europe was torn apart by dissension and destruction. There were intervals of hope and advance but with the rise of nationalism they became short-lived and less convincing. By the first half of this century they were decisively overshadowed by the two holocausts which devastated the continent. National rivalries, and particularly the resurgent enmity of France and Germany, became a threat not merely to a more hopeful future but to the very existence of the conditions of civilized life. Between 1914 and 1944 Europe by its own dissensions showed an almost single-minded devotion to throwing away the leadership of the world, and to reducing its surviving citizens to misery and penury in the process.

Even when the tide of tyranny had been rolled back in 1945 the prospect which confronted us all was almost the grimmest of our history. Leadership of the West had passed decisively to the United States. But there was a grave question mark over whether she would exercise it with any greater continuing sense of international commitment than she had shown after 1918. Nearer at home the Soviet Union, still rigidly Stalinist, still determinedly expansionist, overhung our devastated lands. Britain, the only West European power to have survived with its regime intact, was exhausted by an unprecedented effort which had at once marked the epitome and the end of its independent existence as a world power of the first order. The tasks of putting Western Europe together again, of giving it the capacity both to survive and to regain prosperity, seemed almost unsurmountable. Apart from the dangers from without, it seemed only too likely that disillusionment with life in war-ravaged economies, without even the perverse stimulus of war itself, would inhibit healthy political development and allow the old enmities to breed again.

The period of recovery from this dreadful phase is the period spanned by the lifetime of this famous Prize. And amongst the Prize's previous recipients have been many of those who did most to bring this resurgence out of adversity. From the core of Europe there are Robert Schuman and Jean Monnet, Konrad Adenauer and Paul-Henri Spaak, to mention only a few. From Britain there was Winston Churchill, and from the United States there was George Marshall. And it was abundantly right, if I may be permitted to say so, that in commemorating this phase, even the most ardent of Pan-Europeans should have agreed on honouring that most notable American

Secretary of State. For we should not delude ourselves into thinking that this recovery could have been achieved without the shield of American support and the generous use of American prosperity. Nor can we avoid the fact that throughout this period, at least until very recently—and I shall return to the change we may now be witnessing—the West has lived under firm American captaincy.

Nevertheless, the past two decades have for Europe been a period of remarkable achievement. Yet they have been marred by two major misjudgements. For the first Britain was responsible. We failed to comprehend the extent to which the war had reduced our capacity for independent action. We believed that victory guaranteed our survival as a great power. It did no such thing. It was not that we wished to contract out of Europe. On the contrary we were profuse in our offers of assistance, both military and economic. But we believed that we could do it from outside. The two British Foreign Secretaries of the early post-war period, one of one party, one of the other, both made major contributions to the recovery of Europe, but both made the error of seeing our relationship with the countries of Western Europe as more akin to that of the United States with continental European countries than to their own with each other. Ernest Bevin was a leading architect of NATO, but kept Britain out of the Coal and Steel Community. Anthony Eden committed British troops to Germany for the rest of the century, but tried to encourage the formation of a European army without British participation, and tragically failed to be represented at the 1955 Messina Conference. These were fundamental errors, for which we have paid dearly.

Then they were compounded by an equal error from within the Six. When Britain changed the doors were not open. The two vetoes of 1963 and 1967 not only imposed a further decade of delay upon our entry. They also devalued the force of the European idea and caused a debilitating ideological split within the existing Community. The visions of the future which emanated from the founders of the European idea and the inspiration which seized those who met at the Hague 24 years ago were not related solely to arrangements between an exclusive group of powers. They offered a new way of learning from the bitterness and destruction of the war years, a new way of transcending the restrictions of national sovereignty. But once these objectives had been set they could not be limited to only six countries without undermining their own basis. It was not possible convincingly to say that national sovereignty was outdated, yet to refuse to let more than a limited number of nations escape from its confines. It could not be claimed that Europe could solve its own problems only on a European basis and yet insist that European countries anxious to join should not be allowed to make a full contribution.

We have survived these misjudgements, the one restricting the scope of European unity in the 'fifties, the other holding back its development in the sixties; and the achievements of the past twenty years have in my view been greater than any realistic expectations of 1950. In essence they have been twofold. They have laid to rest, beyond I would hope any danger of revival, the old Franco-German quarrel which so bedevilled Europe and the world for at least a century. It is a mark of the completeness of this achievement that we now accept it as though it could hardly be otherwise, as though little needed to be done, and forget how much has in fact been accomplished. Yet what a difference it would have made, to our lives and our fathers' lives, if this could have been done 50 years earlier. In any appraisal of the achievements of the European idea it should never be forgotten.

In addition Europe has been made rich. Not only has recovery been complete but standards of material achievement and expectation, widely spread throughout the several nations, have exceeded all previous bounds. The Common Market has brought a high degree of common material prosperity. And with that wealth has come a greater sense of security, both from external and internal threats.

Yet this is not enough. Nor will it be enough merely to

enlarge the existing Community. It cannot conceivably be said that our objectives have all been achieved. Some have not yet even been approached. The new Europe has not yet matched her wealth by her inspiration or her influence in the world. In part this has been because of the pre-eminent position of the United States. We have all of us, inside and outside the existing Community, grown used to being a somewhat ill-coordinated group of junior partners within the Western Alliance. Some have welcomed this role. Some—or at least one—have constantly complained against it, have attempted to stand half outside, but have provided no coherent alternative Now, whether we like it or not, we have to prepare for a change. The Atlantic Alliance will I trust continue. We shall need it for some considerable time to come. But America's role will not be the same. With the massive suddenness which has always been a characteristic of the development of her civilisation she has run herself up against over-commitment and overstrain. This is true militarily, monetarily, politically.

She will remain the primary single power in the Western World. But she will no longer have either the resources or the desire to provide an unchallenged leadership, to be a sun around which satellites revolve. Her ill-fated military entanglement in South East Asia has combined with the decline of her competitive trading performance to produce a qualitative change. We must expect her over the next decade to be far more preoccupied with her own daunting internal problem and to have less energy to spare for those of ourselves and the rest of the world than has been the case for the past generation.

The new European Community must be prepared to fill at least a part of the gap. It will not primarily be a military gap. The greatest challenge to our future security is not whether we can defend ourselves although that, with our allies, we must be able to do. It is whether Western Europe, now emerging as the richest and most powerful trading bloc, can make the rest of the world, and particularly that part of it where poverty is still so grinding as to make a mockery of human existence, feel that our success is the ally and not the enemy of their advance. If we can do this, if we can make European unity an accepted force not only for European but for world progress, then we shall indeed be fulfilling a new leadership role. But if we are indifferent to this challenge then increasingly. as the remaining decades of the twentieth century wear on, we shall find ourselves living anxiously on an insecure pinnacle of wealth, surrounded by an increasingly menacing and embittered majority of the world.

Nor is it only externally that we must infuse the Community with a new spirit. So far, after the first political achievement, its greatest successes have been in the freeing of trade and the consequent stimulation of the vast productive capacity of modern developed economies. But society does not exist only to produce goods. First we must ensure that the increasing wealth is fairly spread, both between individuals and between the different regions of the component nations. I would not be frank if I did not tell you that in Britain the greatest apprehensions about our entry are concentrated amongst those who are worst off. There is a widespread view that it will probably benefit the national interest, but perhaps at the expense of those whose defences are weakest. I believe this view is wrong. But one of the greatest encouragements that the new Community could give to those of us who have fought the battle for entry within the Labour Party would be to prove, and to prove decisively and quickly, that these fears are utterly misplaced.

Second, we need a full awareness of the fact that an increase in the output of goods is by no means always to be equated with an improvement in the amenity of life. Many in the existing Community itself, are taking a leading part in spreading this awareness. Let us join together to ensure that we not only enjoy the benefits of modern technology, but control its menaces as well.

Third, we need a growing concentration on the political content and the democratic control of the new Community. Let the emphasis be increasingly upon the wider-ranging phrase European Community and decreasingly upon the limiting commercial phrase of Common Market. Let us face our political problems together, and let us ensure the harmonization of European policies and not merely the harmonization of European trade. It is fundamental to our purposes that this must be fully compatible with representative democracy. It therefore involves a greatly strengthened European Parliament. At this stage I believe it is more important to give that Parliament some effective work to do, some reality of control to exercise, than to decide exactly how it is in the next phase to be elected.

For the Community, as for the world, the next few years are likely to break more new ground than has occurred in the whole of the past decade. This is not only because of enlargement. Even more perhaps it is because both the problems and the fixed points of the past 25 years are receding. It is no longer a bi-polar world. China alone will see to that. It is no longer a West under a clear-cut American leadership. It is no longer a world in which the developing countries will be satisfied with political independence without economic advance. And it is no longer a Europe in which the primary problems are those of material recovery.

In the past you have honoured many of the great figures who have built up what we have, who have between them dragged Europe out of the slough of post-1945 despond. Compared with them my contribution is likely to be small. But I count myself singularly fortunate to be the first prize-winner to be inscribed on your most distinguished roll as this new period begins.

Inequality at Work

For most of us, work is the central, dominating fact of life. We spend more than half our conscious hours at work, preparing for work, travelling to and from work. What we do there largely determines our standard of living and to a considerable extent the status we are accorded by our fellow citizens as well. It is sometimes said that because leisure has become more important the indignities and injustices of work can be pushed into a corner; that because most work is bound to be pretty intolerable, the people who do it should try to compensate for its boredoms, frustrations and humiliations by concentrating their hopes on the other parts of their lives.

I reject that as a counsel of despair. For the foreseeable future the material and psychological rewards which work can provide, and the conditions in which work is done, will continue to play a vital part in determining the satisfaction that life can offer. Yet only a small minority can control the pace at which they work or the conditions in which their work is done; only for a small minority does work offer scope for creativity, imagination or initiative.

The Labour Movement was founded, not only to fight for better material conditions, but to fight against a social philosophy which regarded working men and women as adjuncts of the machines they tended rather than as human beings. The consequences of that philosophy are all around us still. Inequality at work and in work is still one of the cruellest and most glaring forms of inequality in our society. We cannot hope to solve the more obvious problems of industrial life, many of which arise directly or indirectly from the frustrations created by inequality at work, unless we tackle it head-on. Still less can we hope to create a decent and humane society.

The most glaring inequality is that between managers and the rest. For most managers, work is an opportunity and a challenge. Their jobs engage their interest and allow them to develop their abilities. They are constantly learning; they are able to exercise responsibility; they have a considerable degree of control over their own—and others'—working lives. Most important of all, they have the opportunity to initiate.

By contrast, for most manual workers and for growing numbers of white-collar workers, work is a boring, monotonous, even painful experience. They spend all their working lives in conditions which would be regarded as intolerable—for themselves—by those who take the decisions which let such conditions continue. The majority have little control over their work; it provides them with no opportunity for personal development. Often production is so designed that workers are simply part of the technology. In offices, many jobs are so routine that workers justifiably feel themselves to be mere cogs in the bureaucratic machine. As a direct consequence of their work experience, many workers feel alienated from their work and their firm, whether it is in public or in private ownership.

Rising educational standards feed rising expectations, yet the amount of control which the worker has over his own work situation does not rise accordingly. In many cases his control has been reduced. Symptoms of protest increase—rising sickness and absenteeism, high turnover, restrictions on output and strikes, both unofficial and official. There is not much escape out and upwards. As management becomes more professional —in itself a good thing—the opportunity for promotion from the shop floor becomes less. The only escape is to another equally frustrating manual job; the only compensation is found not in the job, but outside it if there is a rising standard of living.

We face a serious problem of strikes and inflation. Since 1966 the number of days lost has risen year by year. Since 1968 the rate of inflation has been rising. But it is only in the last two years that both have escalated out of control. In 1971 more than 13½ million days were lost through stoppages. More than this number were lost just in the first five months of 1972. These are numbers unknown since the days of the General Strike in 1926. At the same time money earnings have been going up fast. During the past two years—despite reductions in overtime—they have been rising at the unprecedented annual rate of more than 12 per cent.

But the increase in living standards during this period has certainly not been unprecedented. It has indeed been unusually sluggish. Wages have merely been running a hard-fought race with prices. It is nonsense to say that wages have been the only factor in the inflation. The movement of house prices, where wages have played very little part, is a clear example the other way. Without a rapid rate of recent wage increase, indeed, there would have been substantial falls in real purchasing power, with a further depressing effect upon the already depressed economy. At the same time it is clearly the case that we could not expect to return to anything like price stability without a reduction in the rate of money wage increase. And it is equally true that the pattern of the past two years has not brought much satisfaction to anyone.

Strikes dominate much of the news. The Government uses them as an excuse for most of its other failures. The nation is impatient and looks for quick and universal remedies. I do not believe that such remedies are easy to find. Some strikes there will always be. Industry cannot be free of a degree of conflict, and such conflict is bound occasionally to find its expression in the traditional democratic right to withdraw labour. But if strikes are sufficiently widespread and continuous as to cause major national dislocation and frequent and widespread inconvenience they are an expression of something deeper than this occasional inevitable conflict.

The Government's solution is to try to prevent strikes by force of law. Yet its Act has clearly made matters worse and not better. The imposition of the railway ballot was a classic example of the foolishness of ill-considered interference. The Court of Appeal decision in the case of the container disputes has shown that even lawyers cannot agree upon the interpretation of some of the most fundamental sections of the Act. The Industrial Relations Act will be repealed by a Labour Government. But the mere slogan of repeal will not be enough. This would leave no framework of industrial law, and less protection than the unions have had since 1875. But I no longer believe that we should expect much from the law in this field. It can too easily make an ass of itself. Industrial Relations law should be used to provide the framework to enable collective bargaining to operate smoothly. It must not be used coercively to try to impose solutions which cannot be reached by negotiation and conciliation.

Industrial unrest on the scale which we are experiencing is a symptom of a fundamental malaise in our industrial society. The time has come for a clear look at the more underlying causes of the unrest. Why do conditions of life in industry produce a climate of mounting discontent? Why is the will o' the wisp of rising money wages, even if this involves rising prices, without any corresponding real advantages, and indeed with the considerable disadvantages of moving workers into higher tax liability, so superficially attractive?

We will not answer the first question without facing head on the inequity and dismalness of the work scene which confronts the majority of citizens. Most work in modern industry is monotonous without being relaxing. The pace and noise of work, particularly in mass production factories, imposes a high degree of nervous strain. The material reward is significantly greater than a generation ago. But the job satisfaction is neg-

ligible. And there is little of the discipline of hope, which is
an essential ingredient of life for the professional and managerial classes. It is a very strong general rule of life that the
satisfaction of a day depends considerably on the prospect for
the next one. The week-end looks better on the Friday evening than on the Sunday evening! The beginning of a holiday
is generally the best part. The sweep of middleclass life, open
admittedly to chances and setbacks, is in general well-geared
to the need for the future to assuage the difficulties of the
present. Rewards and influence tend to expand over the four
decades from twenty to sixty, and sometimes even beyond.
The erosion of life expectation is compensated for by an expansion of the landscape over which the individual can roam.

This hardly applies at all to the manual worker's life. He
has no structure of promotion. His earnings are likely to reach
their individual limit in his early twenties. Thereafter they
can only rise as a result of a general improvement, with which
his own performance will have little to do. By his late thirties
they may even begin to decline somewhat. Nor, in the normal
course, will there be any compensating increase in responsibility. Some argue that for the majority of the population this
is an advantage : they do not want responsibility. I do not believe this. A Norwegian survey has shown that of a sample of
manual workers in seventeen different firms, 90 per cent
thought they could perform more difficult work; 66 per cent
wanted a higher position; and more than half the manual
workers and two-thirds of the office workers wanted a greater
share in decisions relating to their own work. I do not believe
that British workers have less desire to exercise their talents
and initiative than have Norwegian workers. Nor do I believe
that they have less desire to escape from a plateau gradually
tilting downwards.

It is not even as though conditions of working life upon the
prospectless plateau were made cossetting even if unstimulat-
ing. To buttress the lack of job interest there is also an absence
of status, and the flexibility and consideration which goes with

status. Only 20 per cent of manual workers are able to take
time off with pay for personal reasons—as against 93 per cent of
senior managers. Only 6 per cent of senior managers have to
clock on or book in, but 98 per cent of manual workers do
so. Manual workers are much less extensively covered by employers' pension and sick schemes. And their earnings fluctuate
much more, often for reasons quite outside their control. Injustice shows its face, and appears just as inescapable, as
strongly in industry as in other facets of life.

How far is it inescapable? To some extent, no doubt,
monotony and even harshness are unavoidable. But by no
means wholly so. How can the position be improved? I begin
with what is I believe a limited but more important point
than it may at first seem. It is not only strikes which have
been increasing in recent years. The number of days lost each
year through certified sickness has risen from less than thir-
teen on average for each man ten years ago to seventeen in
1968-69. (There are no more recent figures.) Reported factory
accidents rose from 190,000 in 1962 to 269,000 in 1971. Trends
in uncertified sickness and other absences move still more
strongly in the same direction. This is not just a haphazard
development. It has been known for many years that sickness
and accidents—even major certified sickness, and still more the
odd day off because of colds or minor injuries or depression—
are ways of resolving the intolerable stresses which people encounter at work. When work becomes unbearable, a day off,
even with financial sacrifice, provides an essential safety
valve.

Yet some of the aspects of work leading to unnecessary
physical stress are relatively easy to modify. In construction
and shipbuilding, many who work in exposed conditions could
easily be protected against the worst excesses of the weather.
In many factories, shops and offices there is inadequate heat-
ing; others are intolerably stuffy. There is no minimum legislative provision to cover such conditions, nor any legislative
protection against intolerable noise levels. The factory inspector-

ate is so small that compliance with even such regulations as exist can scarcely be enforced.

Industrial health regulations still lag behind understanding of the causes of industrial diseases. Penalties for infringement are derisory and enforcement procedures are often inadequate. Yet why is so little effort devoted to prevention of illness and accidents? The Dale Committee advocated an occupational health service—in 1951. There has been no comprehensive response. Nationalized industries and many of the better-run companies operate their own occupational health services. Why should workers in other companies not receive comparable benefits? An occupational health service, established in partnership with industry and operating under the new Area Health Boards, would fill a major gap in health care and preventative medicine. The next Labour Government must ensure that such a scheme is introduced.

My reason for discussing industrial health is not just that it is an important problem in its own right. It is also a clear example of injustice between those workers with 'progressive' employers and the rest, and an example where there is clear scope for action to alleviate the injustice. It is an example of an area where we—as Government, as Trade Unions, as managers—have failed to act.

But it is not an isolated example. There are other areas, other groups of workers which face especial difficulties and injustices. Disabled workers, for example. They prize the opportunity to work more highly than any other group. Yet, in April 1971, 12.6 per cent of those on the register of disabled persons were unemployed—almost four times as high a proportion of unemployed as in the labour force as a whole. Only about one-seventh of these were special conditions of employment cases. The remainder could be employed in normal jobs—if only employers would take them on. But less than three-fifths of employers were fulfilling their statutory 3 per cent quota of registered disabled employees. Again our failure to enforce regulations which already exist is totally inexcusable.

Some of the worst injustices are found in the treatment of women at work. Most women today will have spent at least thirty years at work before they reach retirement age. Yet the opportunities for them to hold jobs which require much training or receive high pay are very limited. About one-quarter of the workers in the engineering industry are women—but in 1970 there were only 110 female apprentices to skilled craft occupations, and more than 112,000 males. The number of girls and women receiving training of any kind was less than a half of one per cent of the number of boys and men. In industry as a whole, only 7 per cent of girls take up apprenticeships. Forty per cent of boys do so. Women provide less than one-fifth of managers of all kinds, and less than one-tenth of foremen and supervisors, except for superintendents of typing pools.

Even in education, traditionally a field where many women have been employed, there are relatively few women in top jobs. In primary schools, three-quarters of the teachers are women, but only about two-fifths are heads. Much more strikingly, only forty-four of the more than 3,000 university professors in 1969 were women. And although 40 per cent of civil servants are women, they comprise only 6½ per cent of those in the higher administrative grades. These are occupations in the public sector, where overt discrimination is frowned upon, and where women already receive equal pay. But on average, pay for all women has stood throughout this century and longer at about two-thirds that of men. Although our Equal Pay Act should narrow this difference over the next few years, while there are still special 'women's jobs', while women are still on average worse educated than men and while they have fewer training opportunities, we cannot expect that the narrowing will be very great.

An important next step in improving the position of women will be to legislate against sex discrimination in employment, just as we legislated in 1968 against racial discrimination. But beyond that there will have to be continued vigilance by unions. Still further beyond, we shall have to work consciously to change those deep-rooted attitudes in our society which allow many people to pretend that women ought not to have a wide range of choice in the way in which they spend their lives.

Discrimination on grounds of race has some of the same features as discrimination against women. And it has some especially dangerous ones of its own as well. We already have the legislation to outlaw it. But the need for continued vigilance to make sure that the legislation is enforced, the need to change deep-rooted attitudes and the need to make sure that immigrant children remain in education and go on to further training is essential if we are to avoid the evils of a divided society.

Anyone who migrates to a new society competes for jobs from an unequal position—simply because he is an 'outsider' For many jobs, the inequality is shortlived. For others, it lasts longer. For a few jobs, it can be a long time before the migrant can compete from a position of equality. This is especially true where language is a significant factor.

On top of the commonplace disadvantage which immigrants in any society face there is of course, racial discrimination— the crude, irrational, less favourable treatment of people because of the colour of their skin or where they come from. We have a law which prohibits racial discrimination in almost all the significant areas of life. The Race Relations Board suggested in the summer of 1972 that it is not enough to rely on people complaining of individual acts of discrimination. The Board wants to be able to act without waiting for complaints. Their job is to protect the public interest in a particular field, and they have told us that they need further powers.

But no legislation or Board can do the whole job of securing the abolition of racial discrimination in employment and the establishment of equal opportunity. The Board have always said —and I agree with them—that management and the trade unions can have a much more significant effect than the Board can hope to have. Racial discrimination mirrors other forms of discrimination. There has undoubtedly been progress in the past few years, but certainly not to a degree which justifies any complacency.

Government can legislate against discrimination in its various forms. With union help and adequate inspectorates it can ensure that its regulations are enforced. Acting directly, it can do a great deal to improve the wider framework of industrial life.

It is less easy to improve those parts of working life where generalized standards or conditions cannot be laid down. There is often real scope for redesigning the work pattern so that there is more opportunity for individual initiative and a somewhat more satisfying job. A classic case of this in coal mining was documented by the Tavistock Institute about ten years ago. Shifts which had hitherto been wholly separated were given a group identity and more varied work. Other examples are in the assembly of bicycles in this country and of cars in Sweden. It makes a lot of difference if workers can see the end product, instead of only a meaningless bit of it. The results can be dramatic.

Redesign of work presents a considerable challenge to managers, workers and their representatives. It can be creative and continuing, but it would be foolish to pretend that all work can readily be redesigned. Sometimes neither workers nor management want it. Even where they do, it does not follow that there is a solution which is readily acceptable to both sides. Yet participation in the detailed design of their own jobs is fundamental to improving the working life of those in industry.

The basic objectives must be to increase the influence of workers on matters which concern them as individuals or in small work groups, and on matters of company policy in general. It is to wider matters of corporation policy that German and Yugoslav experience, and experiments in Norway, Sweden and this country have mainly been directed. Scandinavian experience especially shows that worker participation in management is likely to prove ineffective unless it is accompanied by workers' control over matters which concern them more directly. Naturally enough, workers are most interested in taking part in decisions which so affect them. Only as interest and experience in dealing with basic shop floor issues build up does interest in wider questions grow.

The extension of collective bargaining to encourage industrial democracy at shop floor level presents a formidable challenge to unions, even where management is sympathetic. Yet without it, improvement in more conventional conditions of work is likely to bring little lasting satisfaction to workers and few lasting rewards to management. Improvements should certainly be made, but we must realize that such improvements by themselves are insufficient to redress the injustices facing most workers in this society.

In removing discrimination, in enforcing regulations, above all in extending the control of workers over their work, government action is almost worthless without the active co-operation of the unions. It is essential that these be strengthened so that the area and the scope of collective bargaining can be widened. Only 47 per cent of the labour force is organized. Many employers remain hostile to Trade Unionism. Retail distribution, hotels and catering, laundries and dry-cleaning are occupational areas with a lot of low-paid employees, who could benefit greatly from organization. When the Industrial Relations Act is repealed, we must ensure that workers have a legal right to join unions. Unwilling employers must be made to give unions facilities to organize, and to give them negotiating rights once membership has been established. There will have to be an independent organization to examine bargaining procedures and to make recommendations for improving them. As the TUC has urged, collective bargaining will have to be supported by effective conciliation and arbitration machinery. I welcome the approach to agreement between the TUC and the CBI on this.

But no improvement in *machinery* will enable us to avoid the major workplace issues of wage claims, price rises and low pay. A credible alternative government cannot dodge them. Apart from other considerations the Government itself pays nearly a third of the total labour force.

We can clear some ground for our approach by outlining the different mistakes of the present Government and of the previous Labour Government. The Conservatives have only one basic approach: sit on the public sector. This was unfair ten years ago, and it is unfair today. It is particularly unacceptable at a time when the Housing Finance Bill threatens big, unnecessary increases in council rents and when the taxation policies of the Government are deliberately widening the gap between rich and poor.

It is also ineffective. Almost every public sector wage claim becomes a test of the Government's will in a confrontation with the unions involved. There is no machinery for identifying exceptional grounds for a pay increase except the brute force of industrial power. Each defeat throws the policy into disarray, while each so-called victory is a simple act of discrimination which stores up trouble for the future.

The main fault of the Labour Government was that we made incomes policy too much of a short-term auxiliary to other economic objectives—first a prop for an unrealistic exchange rate and then a weapon to secure the essential but belated turn-round in the balance of payments—rather than as a longer term contribution to social justice. We also concentrated rather too much attention on the enactment of a series of legal controls.

Nevertheless we should not exaggerate the failures of the past. We had to operate in 1968 and 1969 in circumstances which permitted hardly any increase in consumption. But despite the effects of devaluation there was much less inflation than in the two years we have just lived through. But it was perhaps in the first eighteen months of the last Government that the most pioneering work was done, pioneering work which might have had very beneficial long-term results if it had not been followed—which it need not have been—by the tunnel of exchange rate difficulties. At the start, the Prices and Incomes Board was operated by consent of all the parties concerned, and was accepted as an independent means of investigating the merits of particular pay claims and proposed price increases. It conducted examinations in depth. Its work has been widely respected and studied in other countries.

There are two points to be noted here. The first is that inflation is highly inequitable. It both arises from and exacerbates the injustice of reward. What inflation does is to transfer purchasing power from the weak to the strong. The strong set the pace, and while they remain ahead they derive a real benefit from the inflationary situation. It is not only those who receive large increases in pay who gain; it is those who own houses rather than renting them; it is those who can borrow large sums of money at rates of interest which often become zero in real terms; it is those who are relatively rich and secure already. Thus any policy to combat inflation must combat inequality wherever it is found—and one prong of such a policy must be to prevent those already well-placed from becoming still better off.

The second point is that consent is of vital importance. It is a basic requirement that we must work out conditions between the Labour Party and the unions which are acceptable both to the worker on the shop floor and to the consumer at the shop counter. Neither the trade union movement nor a Labour Government can fight this incomes policy battle alone. But if we want to see a successful Labour Government there is no room for unilateral vetoes either.

It will be an essential foundation of such a basis of co-operation that the prices side of the bargain must be kept. We must therefore be prepared to establish controls over key prices which significantly affect the real income of wage earners, particularly the low paid. Of course it is no use pretending that price restraint on its own is sufficient. The practical difficulties of enforcement and quality reductions are well known, but so are the effects of the inflationary disease—and everyone agrees that the disease has begun to engulf the world in the past few years. When a Republican government of the United States is prepared to lay down 'fair prices' for a wide range of goods it is ludicrous to dismiss price intervention as left-wing bureaucracy run mad.

In the first two years of the present Government the retail price index rose by an unprecedented and unacceptable 17%. Yet within this index the prices which rose most of all—by 32%—were public sector prices. A determined prices policy must take a quite different approach to rents from that of the Housing Finance Bill. This Bill gives a totally unnecessary and government-imposed twist to the inflationary spiral.

Food prices are particularly important to lower paid workers, who spend so large a proportion of their income on food. Here I want to repeat that my commitment to entry into the EEC does not and has never included support for the present form of the Common Agricultural Policy. As the number of farmers in the EEC diminishes and as their farming becomes more efficient—and both of these are happening rapidly—so the EEC interest in agricultural protection diminishes. There are already in Europe strong voices—mainly but by no means exclusively on the Left—arguing for cheaper food. Our voice must be clearly heard in this chorus of reason.

Price restraints raise the question of what powers we require behind an incomes policy. The answer is as little as possible. The law can easily become an unnecessary entanglement. The issue really revolves around what is required by those groups who co-operate to ensure that they are not unfairly treated in relation to those few who insist on standing out. By far the best solution would be for it all to be done voluntarily. The unions could do a great deal amongst themselves. The fundamental discussion about why a long-term voluntary incomes policy is necessary both to secure social justice and hence to combat inflation can all too easily be diverted into the blind alley of short-term bickering about the relatively minor role which the law should or should not play.

Much more important would be the other measures which a Labour Government could offer to eliminate injustice. It should offer a policy to eliminate the worst poverty and to remove the grave injustices of the poverty trap. Many of the poor are not in the labour market; discussion of the tax and social security measures to help them belongs in another essay. But one essential part of this policy belongs here; the elimination of poverty amongst those at work. Many of the low-paid work in firms and industries where trade unionism is either weak or non-existent. Although legislation to encourage the extension of collective bargaining will help, the task ahead of the trade union movement in raising rewards in badly paid and poorly organized sectors is so vast that it would be complacent to expect collective bargaining alone to solve the problem of low pay. In any case, collective bargaining alone cannot be expected to solve the problem of low pay for the worker with many dependants; a minimum wage high enough to meet his needs is far higher than that required by a single worker. The Government must play its part in eliminating poverty by ensuring that allowances for children and other dependants are large enough to allow the family man with fairly low pay a standard of living which does not differ greatly from that enjoyed by his single colleague. But minimum rates of pay themselves are often too low. They have not been subject to direct government action in this country. Where union organization is weak and where Wages Councils are non-existent or ineffective, there is nothing to stop employers paying scandalously low rates of pay for each hour's work. About one-third of women received less than 35p an hour in April 1971—less than £14 for a full working week of forty hours. Such 'sweated labour' is a disgrace to our society.

Only a National Minimum Wage can end such exploitation directly. It carries both opportunities and risks, although many other countries have seized the opportunities without succumbing to the risks. Opportunities because it would say for the first time in Britain that no employer can exploit the under organized by paying disgracefully low wages. A risk, because it would be highly inflationary if all better paid workers were to demand and obtain a compensatory increase to restore their differentials. I support this measure in the belief that this need not happen. The national minimum could be introduced at a relatively low level and then raised steadily in a determined attempt to raise the lowest earnings faster than the average. There is an argument that there would be immediate pressure for an upward adjustment in wage structures as a whole so as to render the whole exercise largely nugatory. The pessimistic view ignores the traditions of concern for those less well-off which can be mobilized in the British trade union movement. We have seen these traditions at their best in the sacrifices which faceworkers in the mining industry have accepted to help their lower paid colleagues. An egalitarian incomes policy could reinforce and work with this concern.

The central object of an incomes policy must be to produce a more just society. That cannot simply be left to happen. The natural economic forces work in the opposite direction. And when the traditional ones are buttressed by the continuing wave of inflation which now affects most of the world, but particularly this country, the results are likely to be still more haphazard. I do not believe that we will get social justice without stopping inflation. And I do not believe that in a modern democratic society we can stop inflation except as part of a powerful drive against injustice.

I also believe that such a sustained policy cannot work without a high degree of acceptance from both workpeople and union leadership. That will be far more likely to be forthcoming if the aim is clearly perceived. The central purpose must not be to get any government out of a short-term economic difficulty. Yet if the acceptance of the long-term aim is secured the chances of avoiding such short-term difficulties are greatly increased. And that avoidance is by far the best guarantee against future governments being forced to lurch into far less acceptable policies. That is the essence of the message we must seek to get understood.

Of course a policy for incomes cannot be expected to provide the whole thrust of the drive for social justice. Any equitable society must include a policy for high incomes as well as for the normal run. High negotiated salaries can be brought within the framework of whatever incomes policy institutions are set up. But most really high incomes are not of this kind. They derive from the ownership of wealth. Hence it is mainly fiscal measures, not incomes policy measures, which must be used to ensure that the rich contribute to society according to their means.

I wrote in the first essay that 'the social forces that bolster inequality are immensely powerful and immensely persistent'. Nowhere is this more true than in the nature of work and the rewards from work. Nowhere is it more important that we should correct these forces.

D

Cities are for People

This essay is about the difficulties of urban living: transport, planning, land use, housing. 'The problem of the cities' has for a decade or more been generally accepted shorthand for a whole range of American political issues. It has not been so generally used here. Yet the problems are basically the same, although some aspects, notably race and decay at the centre, are more acute there, while some others, notably the inflation of property prices and the vulnerability of the countryside to suburban sprawl, are worse here. In both countries there is now a clear likelihood that, without new policies, the future for city dwellers, while it may be one of increasing nominal affluence, will still more decisively be one of declining real amenity. Income and possessions may rise, but the frustrations of life will rise still faster and the satisfactions of life will become more elusive.

This is the more serious as Britain is now overwhelmingly urban. While the rural population has hardly changed since 1750, the urban population has grown from 2 million to 40 million. In 1688, there were more than half a million people in London, but no other town had more than 30,000. Today, about 13 million people live in the London Metropolitan Region, and almost 80% of the population live in towns, or cities, or suburbs.

There have always been technical limits on the size of the city and the spaces between cities. The Romans in the earliest recorded system of regional planning sited their provincial cities

30 miles apart, because a city could and should live on the food brought in from a fifteen mile radius. Until the late nineteenth century, the absence of cheap transport limited the size of cities like London and Paris so that nearly everyone was within a couple of miles of his work, and many much nearer. Population increase was met by overcrowding rather than by building further out. Only the fairly rich could afford to ride from outlying villages like Hampstead or Wimbledon, where they could buy large houses and clean air.

Today we can feed our cities from the ends of the earth. The railways at first and then the motor car made us believe we could spread out our living. Instead of crowding into tenements in Bethnal Green or Camden Town, every family could dream of a semi-detached house with a garden in the outer suburbs. For many, the dream became a reality. It is a dream which still exercises its attraction for some who live in much worse circumstances. But for others the isolation from friends and relations, and the difficulties of travelling mean that it is on the edge of turning into a nightmare. And for the nation as a whole there is no future in a process of endless decanting. The countryside will be engulfed and the cities will be desolate.

Where are we going wrong? Why has our planning system been unable to solve the problems of transport, of land use and of housing? It is not difficult to outline the facts. First prices. At the end of June 1972, the typical modern house in London and the South East was selling at £11,000. Only six months earlier its price was £8,800, and 15 years ago it could be bought for only £2,500. House prices have risen almost as fast in the rest of the country.

The prices of the land on which the houses stand has risen even faster. Land costs represent one third of today's high selling cost of houses in the South East; five years ago they comprised only a quarter. Between 1963 and 1970 housebuilding costs in England and Wales rose by 31%—but land prices more than doubled. More recent figures suggest this faster rise for land has at least continued. But at the end of 1970, nearly 25,000 people were in temporary accommodation for the homeless—nearly 13,000 of them in the London area alone. This is only the tip of the iceberg of homelessness. It does not include the many families who move in with their relatives, sometimes dividing up to do so. Families only seek temporary accommodation when they have nowhere else at all to go—yet official sources admit that they are turning away twice as many as they accommodate.

There are still about 1 million dwellings in England and Wales which are unfit to live in. They are probably unhealthy and certainly lack basic amenities. Some of them at least will, on present policies, be with us for a long time to come. The distribution of unfit houses is most unequal—on the latest figures 7% of owner occupied and 2% of local authorities' dwellings were unfit; the proportion in the private rented sector was *one third*.

Yet about 9 million square feet of offices—some 3% of the total—are estimated to be standing unlet, either already built or under construction, in London alone. The shortages of housing and land are not the only problem of our cities. Especially in London, but in other big cities too, the rush-hour scene is of roads packed with cars, each car transporting one driver, burning oxygen and in its place emitting fumes of lead and carbon monoxide. Buses, each carrying 50 people or more, are interspersed within the traffic jam caused by the 10% or so of commuters who travel by car. To deal with these traffic jams, traffic engineers until very recently used without hesitation to propose even more roads. We are spending more than £500 million a year on major roads—more than we spend on building schools and hospitals put together. Urban motorways particularly are destructive of every amenity other than the temporary convenience of the motorist. To build them, we tear down large areas of cities and reduce whole districts of houses and shops to noisy squalor. We squander our heritage—to produce still more cars on the road, more pollution, and as much congestion and as lengthy journey times as before.

This is a costly form of insanity; in a sane world, people would not be homeless while offices stand empty; cities would not be devastated and communities destroyed merely to make it possible to move about a little more easily for a period of only a few years. How with all our advanced twentieth century planning powers and technology, have we arrived at such a sorry condition?

In some ways there has been substantial progress in this century. The jam-packed, disease-ridden squalor which was normal in cities even within our lifetime has largely—though not entirely—disappeared. As Professor Buchanan wrote, 'Planning was born out of back-to-back houses, out of overcrowding, out of privies in back yards, out of children with nowhere to play, out of ribbon development and urban sprawl, out of countryside despoiled and monuments destroyed'. It was born out of a reaction to market forces in the determination of land use. But these forces are immensely strong. They have never been wholly tamed. They are like lions which have had a series of rather apprehensive trainers. At worst they gobble the trainer up. At best they wait until his nerve gives out, and they can do what they like while a replacement is being sent for. Left alone, these forces will produce one great sprawl, neither city nor country, neither field nor place, where life without a car is impossible, yet roads and parking space will take up two-thirds of the area of these non-cities.

Should our priority be to build enough motorways for the cars people will want in ten and twenty years time? Or should we be thinking about the sort of city people will want to live in? To misshape our environment for the future needs of people trying to escape from the defects of our present environment is a vicious circle. Once it was said, when labourers were being thrown off the land, that sheep ate men. Will we now let cars eat men and our cities? First and foremost, people want space to live in at a price they can afford. Families want gardens for children to play in; older people want smaller flats or bungalows near their families and friends; almost everyone likes to live in a 'village' atmosphere, which places everything within his own neighbourhood—shops, schools, pubs, doctor, library, churches and clubs. Mobility is valued, not for its own sake, but for getting to work easily, visiting families and friends, for heavy or special shopping, and for recreation.

If we think first of the community, and only second of the environment in which it lives, then we should concentrate on improving what we have, not destroying rundown housing and shops and decanting the inhabitants elsewhere in the interests of comprehensive development. Improvement is often cheaper too. But it is not enough to ensure a real choice, a social mix. Young married people ought not to be faced with either taking two squalid rooms over a shop in a busy street, or else moving twenty miles away from their families and friends to find a place they can afford—and even that is escaping them as house prices rise.

The problem in London is particularly acute. We may be approaching the point, clearly reached in New York, where few other than the rich or the very poor live in the inner area. It is already hard to retain teachers for London schools or probation officers for London courts because when they want families they can find nowhere adequate to live. If we can provide housing of varied standards and prices near to the areas where people work, we are not only preserving our cities, we are also relieving some of the transport problem. If part of our problem stems from mass daily travel, part of the solution is to reduce the need for it, by bringing what people need as close as possible to their homes. But this can be only part of the solution, and a fairly long-term part at that.

In the shorter term, much more drastic measures are needed to prevent the conquest of cities by traffic. We must start by recognising that there can be no place for the heavy lorry and a declining place for the private car in city centres.

The heavy lorry is even more a social menace than the private car. Lorries make the loudest noise, smell worst, and do most to destroy the very fabric of the buildings they pass. 75% of freight is carried by road in Britain; twice as high a proportion as in France and Germany, three times as high as in Holland. In Germany lorries can drive straight onto special trains and drive off near their destinations; container traffic could travel by rail to a far greater extent than it does. It is the hidden subsidy which we all pay to road users which keeps such traffic where it does not belong. We should increase the licence fee on heavy lorries to at least the full social cost of their operation; wear and tear on existing roads, discounted cost of building new roads, and an allowance for pollution. The object should be not so much to tax as to deter. We want a much nearer approach to the continental balance of road and non-road transport. In addition, we should resist the proposed new EEC regulation which is drafted to permit lorries of 40 tons (our present maximum is 32 tons); we should reduce the maximum permissible noise faster than to the intended 89 decibels in 1974; we should encourage research into a quieter lorry and the elimination of diesel fumes. And, most important, we should restrict heavy lorries firmly to a few designated lorry routes. Rather than urban motorways, rather than road improvement between towns, we ought to concentrate on providing bypasses which will keep heavy traffic out of old town centres. In the case of London, there ought to be no question of proceeding with the two inner ringways. The object of a road-building policy should be to keep heavy traffic out of both cities and the small towns, not to get it into them.

I turn now from lorries to the private car. The car has in many ways been a great enlarger of freedom. Before 1914 it merely enabled the rich, who were in any case fairly mobile by train, to make more flexible touring adventures along dusty and unfrequented roads.

In the 'twenties and 'thirties the development of small family cars enormously enlarged the range and mobility of the middle class. A few new arterial roads were built and the country began to take on some of the aspects of a motorized society.

In the 'fifties and 'sixties these processes were enormously accelerated. Car ownership became either a fact or a realistic aspiration for most of the community, and in the second of the two decades there was a more active road-building programme than at any time since the end of the Roman Empire. But the construction failed to keep pace with the congestion. And all future indications now are that, however large a share of national resources we devote to roads, however thickly we allow them to scar the countryside, however deeply we cut them into the heart of cities, we shall never do more than keep a few steps behind the surge of traffic. Roads generate traffic at least as much as they give it space to move.

How do we deal with this problem? We cannot just ignore it, on the ground that any solution is an interference with freedom, for if we do this it will strangle us all. And the freedom to sit in an endless traffic block is hardly the ultimate in human liberty. It will even be self-defeating from the point of view of the mobility of the individual, which was the motor car's great original contribution. The motoring organisations show about as much foresight as those who proclaim the sacred right of non-vaccination while a smallpox epidemic builds up.

At the same time, we cannot, without being grossly hypocritical, suddenly pretend that the car, so long enjoyed by a large minority, has now become the most dreadful and socially reprehensible drug because it has spread to a majority and beyond. Those who have had cars for years are not going to give them up. Still less eager to do so—and quite naturally—would be those who have just achieved one after a long period of effort and expectation.

If however we cannot and should not restrict the ownership of cars—except by the indirect method of keeping or creating enough alternative transport so that those who do not want them are not pushed into reluctant acquisition—we shall not be able to avoid some restriction on their use. I am not greatly attracted to a straight pricing device, which will merely substitute minority use for the old solution of minority ownership. Nevertheless, it is at commuter car traffic that the attack must be mainly directed. Apart from a few holiday jams it is that which causes the worst congestion. And it is also the form of car transport which gives the least pleasure. There is no flexibility and little freedom in driving each day down the same jam-packed road to work.

If the roads to city centres were freed of private commuter traffic and parked commuter cars, we could run far more efficient conventional public transport services. With faster, more frequent buses, the commuter would have a journey as short or shorter than he has now, and rather less wearing. Provided there were large car parks at outlying bus terminals, his journey door-to-door would not become worse than it is. Better bus services must also be supplemented by better commuter trains. To support these, particularly where new lines are involved, requires a large flow of traffic, but a recent survey has indicated that Manchester could profitably build a semi-underground commuter railway. And I doubt if anyone would now seriously question the merits of the new Victoria Line or the proposed Fleet Line.

With quicker routes and more use, public transport costs would be helped. Even with present financial targets, fares would rise less. But present financial policies require bus companies and British Rail to break even. The one exception is that British Rail receives subsidies for certain lines on social grounds. But no transport undertaking is allowed to take account of the environmental benefits, which increased use of public transport can bring. The general principle that the polluter pays for the damage which he causes, has not been applied to private road transport. The car and the lorry receive a huge concealed subsidy from us all; railways and buses should be allowed to take this into account. Public transport *ought* now to be subsidised not by accident and with regret, but as a deliberate matter of public policy. The paradox is that if more frequent, faster, cheaper public transport was introduced, the services might come nearer to paying their way. But this does not weaken the argument that the balance between public and private transport cannot be struck unless we consider all we have to gain by cutting down on noise, on the stink of exhausts, on thousands of homes being torn down for spaghetti junctions, on too many people being made to move so that people may move more easily.

To supplement good public transport we must discourage cars from entering or stopping in city centres by having far more stringent parking regulations. No planning permission for car space for shops and offices in cities should be given at all. I believe for example that the scheme to provide a multi-storey Parliamentary car park under New Palace Yard should be abandoned. It is thoroughly misconceived anyway. Powers should in fact be taken to change a lot of existing city centre garages to other use. Car parking spaces on the streets should be drastically reduced. Residents would still be allowed to park their own cars nearby, but beyond that the most stringent regulations should be applied.

I do not regard such measures to reduce the use of motor vehicles within cities as any real invasion of human freedom. They will of course be a superficial inconvenience to me as to many others, but it will be a small price to pay in relation to the results for cities either of strangulation or of destruction by urban motorways. Many think of London—at any rate the more prosperous parts of it—as having been more agreeable a generation or more ago. If so, they had better be prepared to get about it more as their forebears did then.

At present those who do not own cars are finding it increasingly difficult to travel at all, while those who do own them travel slowly through congested streets, creating noise, smell and hazard for all of us, destroying the pleasure of the places they are visiting, and sometimes the places themselves. Instead I want to make it possible to preserve some car use for everybody who wants it, particularly for social or pleasure journeys where the flexibility of motoring means most, but at the cost of less damage to the surroundings. For these surroundings are the places where people live, and work, and shop, and amuse themselves. We cannot have every place dominated by the means of taking people to and through it. Once transport becomes subordinate to living, it becomes possible to think in terms of planning to create, preserve and enhance suitable surroundings where people can live, work and play. It is often the poorer districts today which suffer most from the demands of through traffic routes; they, quite as much as the more prosperous areas, will gain from policies which restrict the use of the lorry and car.

But if we are to create places fit to live in, we must make sure that houses are provided which people can afford. Local authorities must have enough money to provide or encourage the provision of the facilities which people need. We must beware, too, of isolating housing areas and working areas and leisure areas. As the High Wycombe Society said, 'One cannot zone a steel rolling mill in the middle of a domestic housing area, but it is wrong to be too clinical in separating the various activities of a community. It tends to create an evening and weekend man, a work man, a shopping man, and a recreational man; whereas at one time there was a community of whole men. . . .' Today we see this division of work and life in housing estates far from any other facility; in newly developed town centres which cater only for shopping; in industrial zones sensibly sited well away from housing but also so far from shops that lunch-hour shopping is impossible for their employees. Market forces lead to this. People can only afford to buy houses which are built where land is cheap—and land is cheap only where other amenities are few. Local authorities desperate for increased income let their best sites for commercial uses; rather than libraries and clinics, we see shops and offices—often unlet shops and offices. Sometimes they are unlet because the property developers have overestimated the demand for high rent premises—but sometimes they are unlet because the developers prefer capital appreciation to occupation. Even the Government appears prepared to try to end this scandal, but piecemeal attacks on the property developers' worst excesses are no substitutes for a policy to ensure that land is used for the good of the community rather than to enrich today's equivalent of the railway barons. The Government's late recognition of the scandal of Centre Point in no way compensates for its more important failure to stop the planned destruction of nearby communities like Covent Garden.

We have always maintained in the Labour Movement that the additional values which society creates must accrue to society as a whole; but we have not so far found really effective ways of achieving this aim. The last government's attempt was based on a system of *taxing* increases in land values. But the only practicable way of levying a capital gains tax of this kind is on realisation—when the asset is sold or changes hands. And the predictable effect of such a system combined with General Elections at regular intervals is to reduce the amount of land coming on to the market. Sellers are liable just to wait.

Any policy for land must be as simple and determined as possible, and it must give the impression of as great a degree of permanence and irreversibility as is possible in a democracy. We must therefore attack the problem directly—by forcing owners to release land which the community needs. I suggest here that we consider a system of compulsory purchase by local authorities at nationally laid down 'fair prices'. Government or a government agency would retain reserve powers of land acquisition where individual local authorities were unable or unwilling to use the system—for example in the case of overspill housing arrangements or large developments cutting across local authority boundaries. We already have the compulsory purchase machinery, although it will need to be strengthened. Let the Government now direct its energies into devising a system of *fair prices* for land to keep the costs of new buildings down instead of forcing through so-called fair rents to push the cost of housing up. Such a system would entail a set of prices for different cities and for different zones within those cities. It would involve some initial unfairness between different land

owners, but there will be nothing new about that. The existing system allows mammoth differences in the fortunes of those
whose land happens to be zoned for development rather than
agricultural purposes. And we must weigh proposals for change
against the present system, which is unfair to the community
as a whole—not against some ideal state which we can never
achieve in practice.

If it does not prove practicable to apply some system of fair
prices for land which the community needs—and I accept that
the difficulties will be considerable—then we must acquire development rights to *all* urban land for the state. This in any
case will probably be the ultimate solution. But we want a
speedy interim answer. In either case the cornerstone of our
policy must be acquisition rather than taxation. Two thirds
of Amsterdam is owned by the City Council; it is no accident
that it is among the best planned European cities.

An effective policy for land will reduce the rise in the cost
of new buildings; it should also help to stabilise the prices of
existing homes. But even the most stringent controls on land
prices represent an attack on one front only—and the housing
crisis in our cities desperately needs a determined and con-
certed strategy. A Labour housing policy must ensure that
there is sufficient housing for all to be accommodated at a
reasonable standard; that the housing stock is maintained in an
adequate condition and that people can afford the housing that
is provided. If they cannot afford it there are only two choices;
to lower the standard of housing or to devote a higher proportion of the national income to housing and to ensure that the
money and resources benefit those in housing need. For anyone
who knows or experiences the quality of much housing in our
large cities the first choice is unacceptable.

The most immediate housing problem in these cities faces us
in the private rented sector. The share of total dwellings rented
from private landlords has declined from 49% in 1953 to 14%
today. But this still leaves over $2\frac{1}{2}$ million dwellings—and
while the life of the private housing landlord moves slowly but

not necessarily peacefully towards its end his tenants continue to suffer. It may be argued that we should just let this gradual slide continue—but by doing this we would be inviting these acute problems to continue for the next 15 years or 20 years.

There are two quite different ways of dealing with this problem. There is the general free market approach. Rent controls are progressively relaxed, leading the way to very sharp rent rises for controlled tenants. Rebates paid from public money are then introduced to help tenants pay new rents which they could otherwise not afford. In principle, since letting becomes more profitable, more rented property should become available.

This is a highly theoretical approach. In practice since the supply of both land and housing in our cities is inelastic, increased subsidies go mainly to the landlords and the property companies. The stock of accommodation to let does not increase; rents, prices and profits do.

We are beginning to see this process at work in the older areas of our cities. The improvement provisions in the 1969 Housing Act appeared at the time to be both practical and imaginative. As well as making improvement grants for individual houses more generous and more accessible they introduced the concept of General Improvement Areas; where Government grants are available for planning the townscape, planting trees, and providing play areas and residents' off-street parking. But there is a huge gap in the policy. We must provide not only for houses and their environment but—far more important—for people who benefit from these changes. Who is actually going to live in this desirable new accommodation? Who is profiting most from the public resources which are being poured in?

There is a real problem here. Property prices often double or treble where a General Improvement Area is declared. We get desirable restored houses and tree-lined streets. But we may also get controlled tenants harassed out of their homes and long-established communities broken up as the developers take over I welcome the growing opposition to massive demolition programmes and the concrete jungle which grows in their wake. I welcome the emphasis on renovation, and on fitting small groups of new houses into existing streets and neighbourhoods. But we must now recognise that without the right safeguards the improvement policy can demolish a working class community just as effectively as the bulldozer and the crane. The improvement policy is working for houses and for the city environment—it is not working for the people who must be our main concern.

In the Labour Party our approach must be quite different. We must start with an assessment of the housing which people need and the prices which they can afford to pay. There is no solution which does not greatly increase public intervention. In practice we face the old dilemma of ownership or control. It has proved possible to control rents, but not the quality of accommodation for which these rents are paid. Tough rent controls have led to a gradual decline in both the quantity and state of repair of houses and flats to let.

I believe we must now proceed to the rapid municipalization of what remains of the private rented sector. In any event this will happen over about a generation. There is no reason why tenants should suffer in the meantime. We should buy out landlords of controlled tenancies at a multiple of the present rents. The multiplying factor could be reasonably generous but compensation would be based on this current rent and not on a speculator's price allowing for gains if the existing tenants are forced out or the protection of rent controls is removed. The people who would lose would be those who have bought rent-controlled houses after carefully examining the health and likely will to resist of the tenants—a process most reminiscent of the hangman sizing up the prisoner under sentence of death.

I therefore propose that the next Labour Government should municipalise all private rented property with four exceptions— housing associations, service tenancies, flats and houses above a given rateable value, and tenancies where a landlord is letting out all or part of his own home. I believe that there is no other way of achieving equity between different tenants and between tenants and owner-occupiers in general, and that there is no other way of ensuring that public money and resources actually provide for those in housing need instead of raising rents and house prices and breaking up communities in our cities.

Clearly if local councils are to own a much larger number and greater variety of houses and flats there must be safeguards to ensure that their allocation procedures reflect their their new responsibilities. The present emphasis on council provision for families will have to be supplemented by an imaginative and powerful commitment to provide for the young and the old, single people and students, recent arrivals as well as long-established residents. But I am convinced that a combination of owner occupation with an increased and varied council housing stock is now the only way to achieve balanced communities and a reasonable range of accommodation in the centres as well as on the edges of cities at prices which ordinary people can afford. The policy of massive rebates and subsidies which in practice go straight into the pockets of landlords and developers is far from satisfactory. Control of private rents in so strained and complicated a market can never achieve more than a temporary and partial respite. Only a change of ownership for the great majority of private rented dwellings can now meet the desperate housing need in our cities.

The policy proposals in this essay as is always the case involve money; money from the centre and money from the local community. The first priority must be a redistribution from the national Exchequer to stress areas and whole cities which are cursed with poor housing and an overwhelming need for community services of every kind. But the people who live in our cities must have their say as well—and if we are to maintain viable local democracy and responsible decision-making then we must retain substantial *local* powers over the amount of money to be raised as well as the way in which it is spent.

Local councils now have only one effective means of taxing their electors—the rates. And for sharing the burden of providing community services domestic rates are unfair in two ways. Although not as regressive between different social groups as was once thought, they are unfair between individuals because they are related in only an arbitrary and indirect way on ability to pay. And rates are unfair to the groups and neighbourhoods which need help most because of their lack of buoyancy. Where the decision to 'peg the rate'—on the face of it a neutral decision—has the effect of sharply reducing the real standard of services, the scales are permanently tilted against adequate community provision.

We must have a broader base for local authority finance. Boundary changes which bring most of the suburbs within the same top tier authority as the cities themselves make this somewhat easier. It could involve either direct or indirect taxes. But I am sure we must think in terms of giving the local authorities more financial elbow-room.

These are some of the hard detailed problems which we must face if we are to save our cities and make more tolerable the lives of those who live in them. The city has in the past been one of the greatest glories of civilization. In ancient times the City of David, the City of Pericles and the City of Augustus were all of them expressions of the best that human endeavour could then achieve. In the middle ages the cities of Western Europe provided a setting for the soaring gothic of the cathedrals, and although the cathedrals were sometimes pearls set in mud, they at least provided a focal point and a coherence which was at once ecclesiastical and civic. The baroque city devoted more attention to the setting as opposed to the central jewel. It was a work of art, even if of a somewhat formal character.

Nineteenth century industrialization produced many miles of straggling and sordid streets, but also some fine monuments, a few examples of good planning, and the beginnings of modern civic responsibility. The mid twentieth century has put together plenty of bricks and mortar in Britain. It has cleared most but not all the slums. It has changed the pattern of many cities and made their centres almost unrecognisable. But it has not yet achieved a new balance of values which can add some sense of purpose and personality to the rapidly changing urban scene. Blake wanted to build Jerusalem in place of the 'dark satanic mills'. Our need is to create it in place of the soaring office blocks and the searing urban motorways—and unless we move pretty fast we will have left a discreditable and irreversible legacy to the future.

Policy and Party

This book has two central themes—the stubborn persistence of avoidable deprivation and injustice, and the need for a radical and coherent strategy to combat them. In the earlier chapters I have discussed some, though by no means all, of the uglier features of inequality in Britain, as well as in the world community of which Britain is one of the most privileged members, and I have tried to sketch out some of the policies which I believe to be necessary. But over the months since I began to assemble this book I have become increasingly conscious that it is not enough to formulate policies. Policies to a reforming party are like weapons to any army: and even a well-equipped army can be beaten if it is unable or unwilling to use its weapons properly. If the next Labour Government is to launch a more successful attack on poverty and privilege than did the last one, it will need the right policies, but it will also need something rarer and more elusive. It will need the conscious and active support of a majority of the British people—not just for a fleeting moment in the polling booths, but through all the doubts and setbacks which even a successful Government inevitably encounter.

For a programme of the kind sketched out in this book cannot be imposed on an unwilling society by ministerial edict. In recent months we have seen only too clearly the limitations of such edicts. It will be carried out only if society wishes it to be carried out. If poverty in this country is to be eradicated—and, if at the same time, we are to devote a larger share of our national resources to an attack on the infinitely harsher poverty of the developing countries—the more prosperous half of us will have to sacrifice some of the material prosperity which we would otherwise enjoy. The better off can, and must, contribute more than the rest. Inequalities in the ownership of wealth can, and must, be attacked far more vigorously than in the past. So must the cruel and sometimes degrading inequalities of status and power which disfigure the lives of so many working people.

But none of this can alter the central, inescapable fact that poverty in this country cannot be eradicated unless the majority of the community want it and are prepared to make their contribution. Majority support is therefore the precondition of success. It cannot be cajoled into existence in the three hurried weeks of a General Election campaign. Still less can it be bought by an appeal to self-interest. To win it we shall have to mobilise the idealism and imagination of the British people as no political party has done since 1945. I believe profoundly that the Labour Party can do this before the next election. But we have not done it yet. We have no more time to waste.

The Labour Party came into existence as an alliance between the trade unions on the one hand and the Socialists of the Independent Labour Party, the Social Democratic Federation and the Fabian Society on the other. Both parties to the alliance recognised that, although their ultimate aims then diverged, they could achieve more by working together than by working separately. Their co-operation had its ups and downs: sometimes it was almost torn apart in bitterness and rancour. But in spite of some fierce struggles over doctrine and strategy, the alliance held together. It survived the 1914-1918 war and the Russian Revolution which split every other Socialist party in Europe; it survived the crisis of 1931; it survived the divisions of the Fifties and early Sixties. Through seventy years of social change the Labour Party remained, at one and the same time, the political instrument of the organised workers by hand and brain and the political expression of an ideal of social reconstruction. This was the great, historic achievement of the British

Labour movement—an achievement which no similar movement in the world has equalled, and which no one should belittle today.

For both wings of the alliance are as necessary to each other now as they were when the Labour Representation Committee was founded 72 years ago. A working-class party without a Socialist philosophy could easily become a front for a combination of vested interests. A social-democratic party without deep roots in the working-class movement would quickly fade away into an unrepresentative intellectual sect. But although the Labour Party cannot survive without its working-class roots, it cannot hope to put its ideals into practice as a class party, appealing solely to class interests and class emotions. If it does so, it will cut itself off from many of its potential supporters, who do not identify themselves as working-class or see their problems in class terms; worse still it will betray those whose hope for a fair deal lies in a broadly-based idealistic attack on poverty and social squalor.

In the nineteenth century it made sense to picture a great army of proletarians, with nothing to lose but their chains, doing battle with a small elite of parasites and exploiters. That picture is no guide to the problems we face today. The dividing line between the 'haves' and the 'have-nots' no longer runs between the manual workers and the rest of the community: it follows a much more complex route. In terms of current income, many manual workers are to be found on the 'haves' side of the barricade. Skilled workers in well-paid jobs will not benefit materially from an attack on poverty. Indeed, no such attack can succeed unless a good half of the community is prepared to make a relative material sacrifice. To camouflage this fact with the rhetoric of class war, to pretend that resources can somehow be redistributed in favour of the poor at no cost to the majority, is to pave the way for demoralisation and disillusionment once the attack is launched—and, in doing so, to guarantee that it will fail. Sustained majority support can only be won by telling the truth—by appealing openly and directly to the generosity of all men and women of goodwill irrespective of their economic interests or class positions.

At a deeper and more intangible level, moreover, an appeal to class interest and class emotion is incompatible with the vision of a classless society which has always been one of the chief inspirations of democratic socialism. From the beginning, socialists have fought for a society in which men and women would be judged by their unique qualities as human beings, not by the accidents of occupation or social origin. They have fought against snobbery and deference, not only because of the indignity and injustice they breed, but because they are the outward and visible signs of a mean and degrading conception of human nature. But an appeal to class interest is based, in the last resort, on precisely the same conception It, too, assumes that what matters most about a man is the job he has, and not his qualities as an individual : that the barriers which divide men and women from each other are more important than their common humanity.

In doing so, it helps to perpetuate the divisions which have done so much to disfigure and embitter British society. For a political party does not simply reflect the attitudes of the society around it. The appeal it makes to its members and supporters helps to determine which attitudes flourish and which die out. A nationalist party can keep alive the memory of ancient wrongs, and make it that much harder to cure their legacy. A racialist party can whip up fears and hatreds which might otherwise lie dormant. By the same token, a party that appealed exclusively to class interests and class emotions would be almost certain to keep class bitterness artificially alive—and in doing so to make it even more difficult to remove its underlying causes.

The Labour Party, although the party of the organised workers, has never been such a narrow party. It has proclaimed an ideal that transcended class affiliations, and it has contained men and women of all classes in its ranks.

We must ensure that this breadth of appeal is fully maintained. The present Government, with its regressive fiscal policies, incompetent economic management and crass insensitivity to the feelings of ordinary people, has exacerbated class bitterness in a way we have not seen since the war. In the climate created by high unemployment, unprecedented inflation, large tax reliefs for the prosperous and the operation of the Industrial Relations Act, it has been all too easy to take refuge from the complex and uncomfortable social problems of the present in a nostalgic attempt to re-fight the class war of fifty years ago. In some quarters an attitude has grown up, implying that any action taken by any group of workers is automatically right: that anyone who questions the wisdom of a particular strike or the justice of a particular wage claim is a coward or a traitor: that confrontation is to be welcomed: that laws should only have force for those who agree with them.

The emotions that lie behind this current of feeling are understandable enough, but the current itself can lead us in most dangerous directions. We must be resolved to resist it. Laws cannot be lightly disobeyed. Occasionally it is within the rights of an individual—as with a pacifist defying a conscription act—to say that he finds a particular measure so personally oppressive that he has no alternative but to defy it and take the consequences. That is different from organised disobedience involving those who hope themselves to be able to legislate in the future. Their only legitimate attitude can be one of reluctant, protesting acceptance of the statutes combined with a determination to change them at the earliest possible moment. Anything else is storing up trouble for the future. It is particularly unwise for a social democratic party. The possibilities of social advance by democratic means involve the acceptance by powerful interests of measures, particularly in the fiscal field, which they will certainly not like. They should be given no encouragement to believe that laws can be selectively obeyed.

Nor is confrontation a happy substitute for the often

laborious processes of persuasion and compromise which are an inevitable part of parliamentary government and representative democracy. These processes sometimes seem frustrating and time-wasting. But if we want an example of the incomparably greater disadvantages of allowing communities to become locked into unresolvable conflict with each other, believing that change can only be either effected or resisted by force, we need look no further than Northern Ireland.

Parliamentary government is often far from inspiring. But it is the best weapon we have, both for social peace and for social change. The object of statesmanship must be to achieve the change, in the direction desired by the Government of the day, without endangering the peace. One of the main counts against the present Government is that it has shown no regard for these problems of political leadership, and as a result has so narrowly interpreted its constituency as to endanger the peace without producing the change. It is an experience from which we must learn. A Government without a sense of direction can accomplish nothing. But a narrow Government incapable of understanding the aspirations and fears of those outside its ranks, incapable of the sympathetic insight which is essential to national leadership, will run into a defile of defeat and humiliation. If Mr Heath is too narrow to unite the country, it is the more necessary that we should show, not our ability to put one sectional appeal against another, but our capacity to transcend the factionalism of the last few years.

There are formidable problems in making the processes of government more responsive to public opinion. As the pace of change accelerates, as local authorities become larger and more remote, as industry is organised into larger units, so people feel that they have less control over their own lives, that they are at the mercy of powerful impersonal juggernauts, which may bulldoze their house for a motorway, may destroy their community for a vast redevelopment scheme, or may close their factory following a purely financial merger. A major test of any Government must now be its sensitivity to these widespread frustrations. Otherwise it will provoke stubborn recalcitrance or shoulder-shrugging impotence. Wherever there is a choice, local communities must have more freedom to conduct their own affairs and the individual must be brought closer to decision-making.

One of the greatest difficulties for politicians of all parties is to escape from the confines of their own political world and to see how their actions look to those outside it—either because those others are deeply engaged in other fields of endeavour or because they prefer, for quite good reasons of human choice, to look after their gardens or to run their local football team. Yet the object of democracy must be to represent these people as well as those to whom politics is the core of life. Indeed, without substantial support from them there can never be a hope of assembling a majority.

This tempers the degree of party orthodoxy which can or should be imposed. British opinion does not divide itself into immutable trenches, with everybody firmly dug in to one or the other, and unable to communicate except by bursts of shellfire. It would be a dismal day if this were so, for it would mean that the framework of consent, within which we have long lived, had been shattered. It is also an unlikely day, for even if the consent were to go, it is extremely unlikely that everyone's opinion would ever fall into one of two grooves. Public opinion is not two straight lines facing each other, but a spectrum shading through an almost infinite gradation of view, and complicated by the fact that some who are relatively right or left wing on one issue will jump in a different direction upon another.

The duty of the party system is to impose some sort of order upon this ideological confusion, and to make it possible for effective political action to take place and acceptable political leadership to be exercised. In countries with multi-party systems, the parties can be fairly rigid within themselves in the certain knowledge that no one of them alone will ever be able to form a government and that in consequence there will be need for compromise, probably for too much compromise, when a coalition is patched together. With the British two-party system this inter-party horse-trading system is avoided. But the parties have to provide a broader umbrella on their own, and this means a greater tolerance and a greater ability to provide a home, subject to reasonable respect for the habits of the other residents, for those of quite widely differing views.

The Labour Party's job is to represent the hopes and aspirations of the whole leftward thinking half of the country. Sometimes this 'half' is little less than a half. It is still a very significant factor in the national life. The first task then is to ensure that, even as a minority, it exercises its influence responsibly, and by so doing prepares to turn itself into a majority at the earliest possible date. This is never an easy task. Even in the United States, where over the past 50 years at least, there have been ethnic factors making the left-wing party the national majority party, the Republicans have nevertheless controlled the Executive for almost half the time. In Britain there is not such built-in factor.

Yet the Labour Party is the only practical hope for those who have long been sceptical of Conservatism, and now, after half a Parliament of Mr Heath, see their scepticism turned into dismay. This imposes responsibility as well as giving opportunity. The party is the repository of many hopes, both at home and abroad. In the past few years it has disappointed some of these. There is no need for it to continue so to do. A broad-based, international, radical, generous-minded party, aware of its past but more concerned with the future, could quickly seize the imagination of a disillusioned and uninspired British public. Whatever we do we may win a negative victory at the next election. But what we need is a positive victory. For only that offers the likelihood of full success in government. Only that will enable us to carry through a programme which will give us pride in our party and confidence in our processes of government.

Fontana Books

Fontana is at present best known (outside the field of popular fiction) for its extensive list of books on history, philosophy and theology. Now, however, the list is expanding rapidly to include most main subjects, such as literature, politics, economics and sociology. At the same time, the number of paperback reprints of books already published in hardcover editions is being increased. Further information on Fontana's present list and future plans can be obtained from: The Non-Fiction Editor, Fontana Books, 14 St James's Place, London S.W.1.

All Fontana books are available at your bookshop or news-agent; or can be ordered direct. Just fill in the form below and list the titles you want.

FONTANA BOOKS, Cash Sales Department, P.O. Box 4, Godalming, Surrey. Please send purchase price plus 5p postage per book by cheque, postal or money order. No currency.

NAME (Block Letters) _____

ADDRESS _____

_____

_____

Fontana Politics

Fontana Social Science

Books available include:

African Genesis Robert Ardrey **50p**

The Territorial Imperative Robert Ardrey **50p**

Racial Minorities Michael Banton **50p**

The Sociology of Modern Britain
Edited by Eric Butterworth and David Weir **60p**

Social Problems of Modern Britain
Edited by Eric Butterworth and David Weir **75p**

Strikes Richard Hyman **50p**

Memories, Dreams, Reflections C. J. Jung **60p**

Strike at Pilkingtons Tony Lane and Kenneth Roberts **50p**

Figuring Out Society Ronald Meek **45p**

Lectures on Economic Principles Sir Dennis Robertson **75p**

People and Cities Stephen Verney **37½p**

Fontana Modern Masters

General Editor: Frank Kermode

This series provides authoritative and critical introductions to the most influential and seminal minds of our time. Books already published include:

Camus   Conor Cruise O'Brien   **25p**
Chomsky   John Lyons   **30p**
Fanon   David Caute   **30p**
Freud   Richard Wollheim   **40p**
Gandhi   George Woodcock   **35p**
Guevara   Andrew Sinclair   **25p**
Joyce   John Gross   **30p**
Lenin   Robert Conquest   **35p**
Lévi-Strauss   Edmund Leach   **30p**
Lukács   George Lichtheim   **30p**
Mailer   Richard Poirier   **40p**
Marcuse   Alasdair MacIntyre   **25p**
McLuhan   Jonathan Miller   **30p**
Orwell   Raymond Williams   **30p**
Reich   Charles Rycroft   **30p**
Russell   A. J. Ayer   **40p**
Wittgenstein   David Pears   **40p**
Yeats   Denis Donoghue   **30p**

'We have here, in fact, the beginnings of what promises to be an important publishing enterprise. This series is just what is needed by the so-called "general reader" in search of a guide to intellectual currents that clash so confusingly in a confused world.'

The Times Literary Supplement

Many more are in preparation including:

Fuller   Allan Temko
Eliot   Stephen Spender
Lawrence   Frank Kermode
Sherrington   Jonathan Miller
Trotsky   Philip Rahv
Weber   Donald MacRae

The Fontana History of Europe

Renaissance Europe 1480-1520 J.R.Hale **50p**
The latest addition to the series.

Reformation Europe 1517-1559 G. R. Elton **50p**
'Not since Ranke has any historian described the religious and
political history of Central Europe during the Reformation with as
much insight and authority.' *History*

Europe Divided 1559-1598 J. H. Elliott **50p**
'John Elliott is no ordinary historian. He writes without fuss, but
with a sure instinct for words; he is always in command of his
material; always unprejudiced but never unfeeling. He is scru-
pulously fair in his tight allocation of space, and on every subject
he commands confidence and respect.' *J. P. Kenyon, The Observer*

Europe Unfolding 1648-1688 John Stoye **60p**
'A survey which is the best of its kind available in any language.'
The Times Literary Supplement

Europe of the Ancien Regime 1715-1783 David Ogg **50p**
'An excellent introduction to eighteenth-century Europe.'
The Times Literary Supplement

Revolutionary Europe 1783-1815 George Rudé **50p**
'A thoughtful and thought-provoking book. There have been many
reflections on the French Revolution since Burke's but few have
been as unprejudiced or as wise as Professor Rudé's.' *The Economist*

Europe Between Revolutions 1815-1848 Jacques Droz
50p
A work specially commissioned for the series from a distinguished
French historian.

Europe of the Dictators 1919-1945 Elizabeth Wiskemann
40p
'A model of succinctness and clarity.' *G. L. Mosse, Journal of
Contemporary History*

In preparation: volumes by J. S. Grenville, F. H. Hinsley and
Hugh Trevor-Roper.

Fontana History

Fontana History includes the well-known History of Europe, edited by J. H. Plumb, and the Fontana Economic History of Europe, edited by Carlo Cipolla. Other books available include:

The Nation State and National Self-Determination
Alfred Cobban 40p

American Presidents and the Presidency
Marcus Cunliffe 60p

The English Reformation A. G. Dickens 60p

The Norman Achievement David C. Douglas 50p

The Practice of History G. R. Elton 40p

Debates with Historians Pieter Geyl 40p

Russia 1917: The February Revolution George Katkov 60p

Britain and the Second World War Henry Pelling 50p

A History of the Scottish People T. C. Smout £1·25

Europe and the French Revolution Albert Sorel 50p

The Trial of Charles I C. V. Wedgwood 40p

The King's Peace 1637–1641 C. V. Wedgwood 60p

The King's War 1641–1647 C. V. Wedgwood 60p